ENDORSEMENTS

" Change is difficult. While churches claim they want to change during periods of plateaued or declining attendance, if they don't follow an effective process, they often revert to doing the same old things.

RE-FOCUS is an effective process of helping churches transition from having an inward-focus to an outward-focus, while remaining on point, in mission. What makes this strategy so successful is that it is written by someone who has successfully led churches in this transformational journey. My friend, Dave Cole, not only offers great concepts and information, but he brings a wealth of experience in seeing churches reach their redeemed potential. You and your church will benefit from the principles presented in RE-FOCUS."

DOUG CLAY
Assemblies of God General Superintendent

" Dave's focus in the book Re-Focus is a most welcome addition to the myriad of books on missions, leadership, and reenergizing stagnant or dying churches. The practical application tools are valuable, and the illustrations have great merit. John Stott said, 'We must be global Christians with a global vision because our God is a global God.'"

GREG MUNDIS, D.MIN
Assemblies of God World Missions Executive Director

" If you want to learn how to refocus a church, it's best to learn from someone who has walked that path. I have observed Dr. Dave Cole's leadership for nearly four decades, and he knows how to help others refocus because he has done it himself. I watched him lead a refocus effort in a semi-rural church, taking it from 12 people to over 400 in attendance, and for the last 15 years, I have watched him help other churches in our region refocus their missional efforts as well. Dave understands leadership, culture, strategy, and a host of other issues, but more importantly, he walks close to Jesus and loves pastors. Read this book to refocus. Read this book to help stay focused. Read this book to grow."

DR. DONALD E. ROSS
Network Leader, Northwest Ministry Network and author of *Turn-around Pastor*

" In his book, RE-FOCUS, Dave Cole becomes a virtual consultant for you and your leadership team. He offers local church leadership a solid biblical foundation for outward-focused ministry. He then goes a step further and gives practical direction to help leaders implement (or re-establish) outward-focused ministry. Not only is the book biblical and practical, but it is powerful because it is a reality for the author. Dave and his wife, Debbie, live outward-focused lives, and they are helping churches join them on the outward-focused adventure."

TOM JACOBS
Superintendent
Iowa Ministry Network

" I love Dave Cole's heart for the Kingdom, for the Church, and for reaching people for Christ - he's one of the great visionaries and innovators when it comes to church leadership in our day. Growing out of his own incredible experience, RE-FOCUS contains insights, principles, and a framework that will propel any church to grow and reach its full missional potential in Christ. It's a clear-minded take on how to reach today's ever changing culture for Jesus."

DR. KENT INGLE
President of Southeastern University, Lakeland, Florida, author of *This Adventure Called Life, 9 Disciplines of Enduring Leadership*, and *Framework Leadership*.

" I remember when Dave Cole came and spoke to our congregation and network churches. It was the first time I heard him present the idea of becoming an 'outward-focused' church rather than an 'inward-focused' church. The term 'inward-focused' describes most of the churches in our nation. I was challenged then, but after reading this book that treats this touchy topic in an in-depth manner, I was challenged in an even greater way. It is obvious Dave has hit a church growth nerve. Here's the good news though. This book doesn't leave you hanging. As a matter of fact, this is one of the best step by step manuals to becoming a Biblically directed and outward-focused church I have ever read. If you are like me and love a book that guides you through the various processes that bring winning ministry results, this book is for you. This is a must read for every church leader who is serious about moving into a new paradigm of ministry for the 21st century.

PASTOR DON JAMES
Senior Pastor, Bethany Church, New Jersey
Assistant Superintendent, New Jersey Assemblies of God

" Pastor Dave is uniquely qualified to speak and write about, "Creating an Outward-Focused Church Culture." Having served as a pastor, church planter, community leader, and network leader; he has led successfully putting into practice the strategies necessary for a church to become an Outward-Focused Church. In his book, RE-FOCUS, he explains how to move a local church that is plateaued or in decline to being strategically missional and creating a cultural change that will stick. Every pastor and leadership team will benefit from the book as well as the workbook. The workbook will help church teams take inventory of their church cultural and define their strategies to accomplish their goals of becoming an Outward Focused Church.

BILL WELCH
Superintendent, Alaska Ministry Network

RE-FOCUS

CREATING AN OUTWARD-FOCUSED
CHURCH CULTURE

Jim + Joyce,

Be blessed as you approach
each day as a blessing
with Jesus!

Dan E. Cole

RE-FOCUS

CREATING AN OUTWARD-FOCUSED
CHURCH CULTURE

DR. DAVE E. COLE

Forward by Rob Ketterling

Outward-Focused Network

Outward-Focused Network
Refocus
Creating an Outward-Focused Church Culture
Dave E. Cole

Outward-Focused Network
P.O. Box 1062
Duvall, WA 98019

Published in the United States by Outward-Focused Network LLC. Designed, Illustrated and Edited by Jon and Sara Wren, Wren Designed LLP,
Snoqualmie, WA.

ISBN-13: 978-1-946210-04-3

All scripture passages taken from THE HOLY BIBLE. NEW INTERNATIONAL
VERSION®, NIV® Copyright © 1973, 1978, 1984, 2011 by Biblica, Inc. ®
Used by permission. All rights reserved worldwide.

Printed by Thomas Shore Publishing, LLC

ABOUT THE AUTHOR

DAVE E. COLE

Prior to becoming a pastor, while still attending college, Dave co-owned and operated a painting company in the Seattle area that grew overnight to become a successful business.

Dave pastored a growing church in East Wenatchee, Washington for 20 years with his wife Debbie. While in Wenatchee, Dave and other denominational leaders helped to meet the needs of hundreds of people every month by creating an outward-focused ministry, *Serve Wenatchee Valley*.

Dave was elected as Assistant Superintendent for the Northwest Ministry Network of the Assemblies of God in 2002, and he continues to work with hundreds of pastors and congregations who desire to move beyond the status quo of church ministry. He recently focused his doctoral studies in developing an outward-focused church culture. Dave serves as Adjunct Professor for Northwest University in Kirkland, Washington.

His expertise in both secular business and the church world brings a wide arena of knowledge and experience in helping organizations and churches focalize from an inward-focused culture to an outward-focused culture.

ABOUT

OUTWARD-FOCUSED NETWORK

Outward-Focused Network
P.O. Box 1062
Duvall, Washington 98019

You can learn more about the author at the following on-line locations:
www.outwardfocusednetwork.com

Facebook: Outward-Focused Network

ACKNOWLEDGEMENTS

I dedicate this book to my amazing wife, Debbie, who eagerly began an outward-focused adventure with me and encouraged me to avoid a status-quo life and ministry. This book would not have been possible without your endless support.

To my exceptional daughters and son-in-laws, Adrian and Ryan, and Shane and Hayley, who blessed me with five wonderful grandchildren: Emery, Cole, Henley, Cade, and Haven. My deepest desire for you is to be about the main thing, and that's Jesus. May He guide you to love Him with all your heart and to love your neighbor as yourself.

To Kathy Jingling and Hanna Lyons for their editor's expertise, and Jon and Sara Wren who spent countless hours illustrating the RE-FOCUS book and workbook.

Table of Contents

– Introduction –

The church faces great challenges in reaching today's secular culture. As churches continue to age, they gradually become inward-focused and can lose the ability to relate with people in their communities.

These churches can pressure their leadership to spend the majority of its resources and time in meeting the members' escalating demands, thus reducing the church's ability to carry out the Great Commission. As a result, nine out of ten churches are declining in America or growing at a slower pace than their communities.[1] Although this statistic seems alarming, hope still exists for the Church.

The solution to transitioning an inward-focused church culture into a life-giving, outward-focused culture requires a number of strategies. Hope comes from looking to an outward-focused God who has been active since the beginning of human history.

Our outward-focused God has pursued people since the creation of Adam and Eve, and continues to encourage His followers to look beyond themselves. God's outward-focused mission began out of His love for the entire human race. His love sent Him on a mission of grace and mercy.

This practical book will guide leaders of any size church to strategically change their church's culture from the status quo of inward-focused ministry to the dynamic of outward-focused ministry and effectiveness of mission.

– Forward –

BY ROB KETTERLING

A t the end of Matthew's gospel, we find one of the most well-known sermons of all time. It is the pinnacle of Jesus' teaching, and it serves as the foundational purpose of the church. The message, while short, gives a clear call with firm direction: GO!

This is not a suggestion or an option. This is an imperative. The Go is the call; The Go is the Great Commission.

When the church focuses on The Go, the people unite. They rally together to accomplish the daunting goal of reaching near, far, and to the ends of the earth. In fact, Jesus distinguishes The Going by the relative distance of the people to whom He was speaking. Acts chapter 1, verse 8, "But you will receive power when the Holy Spirit comes on you; and you will be my witnesses in Jerusalem and in Judea and Samaria and to the ends of the earth."

In this context, Jerusalem is local, Judea is regional, and The Go continues on to the end of the world. As a result, churches and people, whose emphasis is on The Go, reach out in encompassing waves accessing locally, regionally, and globally for the advancement of the Kingdom of God.

To accomplish such a significant mission, resources and talents are pooled together and brought to the table. No longer are our best players reserved for the home team. Our best is sent first in order to accomplish The Go. People give, people are sent, and people go. The cycle repeats itself time after time as the church surges forward to reach every tribe, language, people, and nation.

It is no surprise then that when there is an emphasis on The Go, people go. Short-term missions trips can be a powerful catalyst. Through short-term teams, people experience God moving around the world in ways that often change their own hearts. At our church, River Valley, we encourage everyone who starts attending to go on a global missions trip within their first four years. The fifty teams we will send this year alone are a testament to that emphasis.

The best part about this is there is no prerequisite to go. You do not have to be qualified or prepared; you just have to say yes, and that's biblical! Did you know the first missionary who was sent out was the demoniac called Legion? Moments after Legion's salvation, Jesus tells him to go to the Ten Cities and give a testimony of his salvation. Merely moments before he was naked and possessed; not a whole lot of qualification or preparation there. All that matters is that he was commissioned by Jesus to share his story. He was sent with a purpose.

Indeed, when there is an emphasis on The Go, people are sent all the time! At River Valley, we have a goal of sending 500 missionaries for at least a year to bring The Gospel to anyone who has not yet heard The Good news. I don't care how big your church is, that's a God number! And we are committed to seeing this goal through because we have gone from only a giving church to a giving and sending church. Our people have caught the emphasis on The Go, and they want in!

Families, seniors, couples - more than 150 already have gone. All because the emphasis is on The Go! Churches need to reorient their emphasis to The Go. Jesus, Himself, was the initiator of this emphasis, as shown in The Message's paraphrase of Matthew 9:

> Later when Jesus was eating supper at Matthew's house with his close followers, a lot of disreputable characters came and joined them. When the Pharisees saw him keeping this kind of company, they had a fit, and lit into Jesus' followers. "What kind of example is this from your Teacher, acting cozy with crooks and riffraff?"
>
> Jesus, overhearing, shot back, "Who needs a doctor: the healthy or the sick? Go figure out what this Scripture means: 'I'm after mercy, not religion.' I'm here to invite outsiders, not coddle insiders."

My prayer is that God would help us to focus on The Go, and that He would reorient our churches to this emphasis of inviting outsiders and reaching the least of these. The church was never meant to be inward-focused.

In Dave Cole's new book, *Re-focus*, he takes a real and practical look into this issue of an inward-focused culture found in so many churches today. Dave is not only an experienced Pastor in the local church, but his expertise to discuss church culture at the macro level comes from years working with the Northwest Ministry Network of churches. Learning the ins and outs of churches ranging in size and location has given him a unique and valuable perspective on relevant church culture. He tackles this issue with wisdom and grace. It is an honor to introduce you to someone I know will make a lasting impact on your life and ministry. No matter where your church is in the orientation of The Go, read this book, and let us all reorient ourselves to the emphasis on The Go!

ROB KETTERLING
Lead Pastor
River Valley Church

Chapter 1
OUT OF FOCUS

Recently, after helping our parents move, my brother and I dropped off a few loads at a local thrift store on the Olympic Peninsula.

When we arrived, we pulled up behind a car that had an orange cone in front of it. After five minutes, my brother Doug got out and walked up to see what the problem might be. He approached one of the men working, and was informed that we would have to wait so they could sort the previous load into a semi-truck.

Five minutes later, they allowed us to drive up and drop off our load. It was apparent they were not happy with us. The young man wrote out a receipt for me. I suggested that we keep the receipt open because we would be back. "Well, how much are you bringing back next time?" he asked. I said, "About the same as this load." He shook his head and handed me a receipt.

The next time we came back, sure enough, the cone was blocking our way up the driveway. I thought, "This time, I am going to play the nice guy." I left the truck and walked up to visit with one of the older employees. I commented, "Wow, it looks like you have a lot to sort." He replied, "Yes, and it will be some time before we can help you." I said, "Okay," and thought I would just stand there for a while. Finally, the younger worker came out from the back room with a bottle of water. I said, "We are back." He looked at me and slammed his water bottle down on the counter. I stood in front of him and said, "You know, in Seattle, the workers at our local thrift store are excited to see me, but you seem upset that we are dropping off items. Isn't that what you do? We are trying to be a blessing to the community and it seems like you are ticked off at us."

Here was an organization created to help the community. First, they take the unwanted items off people's hands, and second, sell those items at a low price to people who need it, providing jobs for many people. However, the perception that I received was they do not want my contributions and will get mad when I drop off something.

The young man immediately started backpedaling. He apologized for his behavior and explained that they were having a bad day.

This thrift store's mission statement presented the following ideas: Our goal is to improve individuals, families, and communities lives by helping needy people have opportunities to achieve their full potential through work. It took only two employees to give an extremely different impression.

Two years have passed since our first visit to that thrift store. Within that time, Dad and Mom passed away only ten months apart. Doug and I returned to their house for a final cleaning. There were a number of items we set aside to bring to the thrift store again. Curious as to how we would be treated on our return visit to the same thrift store, we were surprised to find not one cone, but three cones now covering the drive-thru combined with a sign which read, "Forklift Spotter Required. Do not walk up donations. Closed for 15 minutes." Instead of following the mission and eliminating barriers, this thrift store's culture was one of setting up barriers. Over two years, the culture of the organization became increasingly inward-focused.

How does this happen? It can happen in any ministry over time. The longer a ministry exists, the more energy, finances, resources, and care is required for the insiders. Mission fog happens when the organization loses focus of WHY they exist in the first place. The single greatest cause for mission drift is lack of a clear vision.[2]

My wife Debbie and I had the rare opportunity to re-start a church and pastor it for 20 years. Although the church was essentially a church plant, we had to constantly challenge the church to stay on mission as the natural tendency was to grow inward-focused.

For the past 15 years, Debbie and I have been serving our Denominational Network to help churches transition from being inward-focused to outward-focused. We have encountered almost every church culture that exists. A typical scenario for many churches goes like this.

It is early in the fall, people are struggling out of the summer slump, and ministries are bustling in every area of the church. This is the time when attendance picks up and everyone gets excited about a new school year and a new church year. Orientation night for all the children's ministries are lacking a number of families as the soccer, football, dance, and music schedules for school students keeps the parents away.

After several weeks, the numbers still are not bouncing back. It is becoming obvious that numerous families just aren't coming back to church. Sunday mornings, the same empty seats from the summer season are staying empty. There are a few new families who have recently moved to the area. They stop by for one Sunday to see what things are like, but they never return. The leadership assumes that they are not a fit for their style of church.

Months pass and it is pretty obvious the church needs to find another solution to the shrinking numbers. The ministries and activities fail to draw people any more, and the leaders of various ministries are talking about quitting. How did they get so out of focus?

"Roughly three-fourths of established churches in North America are either declining or on a long-term plateau. Such churches are ineffective at making disciples—at least new disciples—and function with a lack of fruitfulness and hope."[3] The dilemma you just read about happens in churches across ministry and denominational lines. In spite of differences due to size, location, or structure, many churches and ministries are struggling with decline instead of growth. Some churches are seriously looking at closing their doors if things do not change. Pastors are bewildered at the lack of consistency in people, but are determined to continue with the status quo, in hopes that things will somehow turn around.

What is the major problem? Many churches have lost their focus. Over time these plateaued or dying ministries became inward-focused.

DEFINING THE TERMS

Let's define the term, *inward-focused*. Every church has a focus or reason for being. Pastors have learned to develop some sort of plan or goals to work toward. They may even have a written missions statement that appears on a wall or in a weekend folder. The truth is, many churches set out to function in a way they believe will enable them to see and carry out God's plan, to "go and make disciples of all nations." Unfortunately, the outward-focused plan of God to reach the world distorts, and a church becomes *inward-focused*.

INWARD-FOCUSED CHURCH: OVER THE PROCESS OF TIME, CHURCHES ARE TEMPTED TO SPEND THE MAJORITY OF THEIR ENERGY AND MONEY TO CARE FOR THE ESCALATING DEMANDS OF THE CURRENT MEMBERS. THE FOCUS OF THE CHURCH GROWS INCREASINGLY SELF-INTERESTED WITH DEMANDS TO INCLUDE CONNECTIONS WITHIN THE CHURCH, DISCIPLESHIP, AND SERVICE MINISTRIES, WHILE A LESSENED FOCUS ON EVANGELISM OR COMMUNITY REMAINS.

A church mission statement can be outward-focused; however, the challenge comes when trying to change the culture of the church from inward-focused to outward-focused.

Another way to see this process is to pause and think about a church's culture. Church culture involves much more than the bank balance, square building footage, and the hired staff. It goes beyond the beliefs and values of a church that are often communicated as its purpose or reason for existence. Culture permeates everything in which the church is involved.

JR Woodward stated, "Culture is like gravity. We never talk about it, except in physics classes. We don't spend a lot of time discussing gravity throughout the day, however gravity impacts everything we do, including the additional wrinkles we find on our faces."[4]

Culture reflects the beliefs and values of a church in the way it functions or develops customs. It reveals the attitudes and the atmosphere of the church community. Another way to identify culture is to ask, "How do members, attendees, visitors, and your community view your church?"

A closer look at a church's culture can be found by watching and listening to how it operates on a weekly basis. Perhaps you have experienced visiting another church and remember noticing the attitude of the people. The décor, the aroma of the church, the way people participate, or the time it takes for people to exit after service, reflect the culture of the church. Church culture can be observed in how the greeters assist others. The culture can be seen in the children's ministry areas, the activities announced from the pulpit, and the language in the weekend folder. Most people have already made up their mind if they will return to a church before the pastor's message is delivered.

DETERMINING YOUR FOCUS

A cultural assessment process is first necessary to begin any cultural transition. Churches that possess a greater self-awareness concerning their culture have greater potential for change. If pastors or leaders do not assess their church, the outward-focused culture can subtlety slide into the background, being replaced by an inward-focused culture. This devastating cultural phenomena is what I refer to as, "Mission Fog."

DISCOVERING MISSION FOG

Take a look at this picture and see if you can detect anything wrong about the boy in the picture.

The picture is me as a small toddler. From the looks of the picture, you would think that everything is going great for this young boy. However, there is something wrong, and it took a few years to find the problem.

I spent my early childhood living in a vision fog due to extreme stigmatism. My parents wondered why I would sit about two feet from our television in order to see it. I thought it was normal. When I colored, I would have to hold my head extremely close to the coloring book. I thought this was normal.

My first grade teacher realized that I was unable to see what she wrote on the black board unless I stood very close. She recommended that my parents take me in for an eye exam. The optometrist had me sit in a chair and he placed a strange machine with a long mechanical arm in front of my face.

The machine had all kinds of lenses attached. He flipped between two lenses and asked which one was clearer. He said, "Here is one, now what about two, which is clearer?" After an extended time of assessing my situation, the optometrist found that I needed corrective lenses. I remember driving home with my mother the day I received my first pair of glasses. For the first time, I realized I had been living in a fog. The brilliant definition and detail in the tree leaves and plants left me speechless. The world became a new place of adventure by correcting my focus.

I had lived in the fog all my life and did not realize that my vision could be any different. With this new understanding, I never started a day without putting on my glasses that gave proper focus.

The problem for many churches is this, they have lived in the fog so long, they believe their inward-focus is normal. This is called Mission Fog and it can happen to anyone and any organization. They lose focus of the vision or real reason for their existence. Instead of continuing the call of reaching the world, the out-of-focus vision blurs into maintenance of ministry rather than clarity of mission.

WE ARE OUT OF FOCUS WHEN WE STRIVE TO MAINTAIN MINISTRY RATHER THAN FULFILLING THE MISSION.

Mission Fog occurs gradually over time by meeting the escalating demands of people already connected to church while losing focus of the mission to reach people outside the church who have not heard the Good News.

DESIRE FOR MORE

The church in America in many ways reflects the culture of America. American culture encourages receiving over giving. The average church member can be inclined to view church from a consumer receiving mentality over a serving and giving mentality. Church members are tempted to desire being served rather than serving. Their individual rights and entitlements are considered more important than sacrifice and they view their tithes as membership dues that bring them never ending privileges and anticipations.[5]

The average consumer shops for the best value and receives more than what they pay for. The wish list on every internet market simply reveals that individuals will not only order great deals, but they also have an ongoing list of desires. This consumer receiving mentality naturally spreads into the church. Ministry slowly shifts from serving to being served.

Countless church members believe the pastoral staff exists to meet all their expectations. They believe the right atmosphere, worship format, ministries, and sermons must meet the needs of those who already attend the church. There is nothing wrong with caring for the members of your church; however, a church that stops here will generally plateau and die. They will certainly fall short of God's intended mission for them.

The newest church statistics reveal that churches in America are dwindling. A Gallup report shows that more people are declining to claim any religious faith even as the numbers of those who declare they are Christians drop annually. Gallup states this trend has been happening for more than half a century.[6] This report should cause us all to stop and assess what is happening with the overall focus of the Church! Studies show that only 15 percent of Millennials, those born between 1980 and 2000, are Christians.[7] Contrast this statistic with the Builders, those born before 1946, of whom almost two-thirds are Christians.

This information should challenge church attenders to look in the mirror and ask the questions, "Am I a receiver or a giver? Are we inward-focused, concerned only about our own needs, or are we continuously outward-focused, carrying out God's Mission?"

DEMANDING THE PRIVILEGES

With clubs, gyms, and many organizations, a membership comes with certain privileges. As long as you pay your dues, fees, or rates, someone will provide all the amenities that are promised. Those privileges include someone serving you. Such places are designed to collect the membership fees, and then employ those who will serve the needs of their members enjoying the amenities. I am also sure that everyone who has ever served in a ministry leadership position can tell of at least one person who seemed to have high expectations they felt justified in demanding.

Maybe you have heard similar statements as listed below?

- "Remember Pastor, we were here long before you came."

- "Since this is my church, I expect to be asked before any changes are made."

- "Don't forget who pays your salary!"

Viewing the church as a club with membership privileges is the opposite of focusing on being a part of a missional community. The entitlement crowd will continue to look for additional privileges they want to claim as their own and find ways to be exclusive from outsiders. Not only do these churches frown upon outsiders, but they also tend to over-emphasize their unified membership. A church that consistently talks about their unity may be masking their lack of outreach. Take a quick look at the list of characteristics that an inward-focused church exhibits as they attempt to deal with their values and rights:

- Being a private club with safety and protection for its members.

- Serving the core constituency.

- Replacing the focus on reaching people who have not heard the Gospel with focus on preserving the present membership.

- Meeting the needs of the members with no idea of the needs outside the church.

DISCONNECTING FROM MISSION

A church loses focus when it lacks mission clarity. No one can remain anchored in the organization's mission, if the mission is not clearly articulated.

CRYSTAL CLEAR VISION IS THE STARTING POINT FOR AVOIDING MISSION FOG. IF YOU CANT SEE WHERE YOU ARE GOING, ANY ROAD WILL GET YOU THERE. [8]

Inward-focused churches prefer the status quo to a biblically missional call. Repetition and stagnation become the norm, as those leading think that if everyone in the church is happy, they are making a difference. Many leaders often take a position of not rocking the boat to keep it from overturning; at the same time, they forget the boat never left the harbor and remains tied to the dock. Instead of missionaries going into the world, the church finds contentment in serving a group of people on the boat. John A. Shedd,[9] wrote,

A SHIP IS SAFE IN HARBOR, BUT THAT'S NOT WHAT SHIPS ARE FOR.

- John A. Shedd

If you have stayed with me so far, please do not give up and think there is no hope for your situation. Just as I found clarity in my vision through the use of glasses, you too can find hope with mission clarity.

Mission clear churches recognize that Jesus is the difference. They articulate the mission Jesus is on and follow it. Mission clarity begins with the willingness of the leader to examine their focus. As a church leader, what motivates you to do what you are presently doing? I want to encourage you to honestly assess your leadership through answering the following questions.

VISION CHECK

1. Would you say your church or ministry would best be described as "in decline," in "long-term plateau," or "growing?"

2. What made you select that description?

3. Write your church's missions statement here.

4. Do you see that statement as outward-focused? Explain.

5. Which indicator of missions fog does your church struggle with the most?

Chapter 2

BIBLICAL FOCUS

The Children's leader was so focused on her young students in their chairs, she failed to see the new mom with her little boy enter the auditorium. They stood in the doorway for some time just watching the presentation, wondering if they should step into the room. Then the leader looked up and noticed her visitors. She wasn't used to someone coming to her door a few minutes after starting time, and she certainly hadn't planned on anyone beyond her regular group of children. Everything was a bit awkward when the leader frowned, knowing there were no spare chairs, crafts, or snacks for extra children. The lesson was about the love of God, but the leader's body language revealed something much different. Somehow the love of God was lost between the lesson and the doorway.

Stories like this take place every weekend in churches around the nation. My wife, Debbie, and I are invited to speak at many churches each year. To be honest, we can relate to the mother in this story. One particular Sunday we pulled into a church parking lot and could not find what door to enter as there was no signage. When we entered the main door, no greeters were present to welcome us. Everyone in the lobby seemed to be having a great time; however, it seemed as though they did not see us enter. We waited for some time, and entered the auditorium. Many people were visiting together in huddles, yet no one acknowledged us. We made our way to the front of the church and sat down without anyone in the church saying hello, and yet we were the guest speakers. The inward-focused culture seemed to have permeated throughout every part of the church.

CLARIFYING THE CHURCH'S CORE REASON TO EXIST

These inward-focused examples certainly do not reflect God's plan for the church. The Bible is quite clear about God's outward-focused love and plan of reconciliation for all. He is an outward-focused God. There are times when the activity of Church can lose a biblical outward-focus.

The propensity for any church to turn inward-focused exists as a real threat to the mission. The longer an organization exists, the more energy, resources, time, and money are needed to care for the insiders.

Simon Sinek, author of *Start with Why*, refers to a concept called the Golden Circle, inspired by the Golden Ratio. The Golden Ratio, from the early Egyptians, was proven, by Leonardo da Vinci, to answer the why, how, and what of organizations.[10] Many organizations find it difficult to express WHY they do what they do. The purpose of asking the WHY question centers on the purpose of the organization, and clarifies the reason for being. Most organizations, over time, work from the outside-in and begin with the WHAT and the HOW of their organization and spend little time on WHY the organization exists.

THE GOLDEN CIRCLE [11]

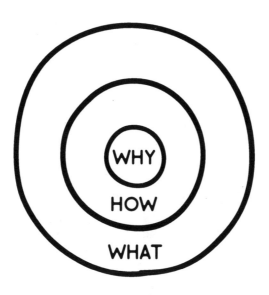

For any organization, mission clarity must be there with an emphasis on the WHY. There is always a need for a clear statement of mission and values which will reinforce the organization's culture and identity. When the Northwest Ministry Network began training Church Planters in 2002, the first instruction began with WHY. Each planter created a missions statement, focusing on the great commission of Jesus Christ. The great commission answers the WHY for the church. Outward-focused churches exist to fulfill the Great Commission, encouraging believers to witness and make disciples of Jesus Christ.

OUTWARD-FOCUSED CHURCHES EXIST TO FULFILL THE GREAT COMMISSION: TO WITNESS AND MAKE DISCIPLES OF JESUS CHRIST

The Great Commission is found in Matthew 28:18-20,

> [18]"Then Jesus came to them and said, "All authority in heaven and on earth has been given to me. [19]Therefore go and make disciples of all nations, baptizing them in the name of the Father and of the Son and of the Holy Spirit, [20]and teaching them to obey everything I have commanded you. And surely I am with you always, to the very end of the age."

A "Great Commission Culture," envisions missions as happening right here at home and across the world simultaneously. This vision will urge a church to look at the big picture that God has in mind. Missions is more than a ministry of the church. Missions is who the church is both at home and abroad.[12]

MISSIONS IS MORE THAN A MINISTRY OF THE CHURCH.

MISSIONS IS WHO THE CHURCH IS BOTH AT HOME AND ABROAD.

Outward-focused churches often include the following core concepts:

- A clear outward-focused theology.

- Investing its resources in those who are not yet part of the church.

- Strategically focusing on attracting new people.

- Constantly assessing what specific things they are doing to reach the unchurched in their neighborhoods.

- Prioritizing activities and ministries designed to reach out to people who are un-churched, de-churched, and unbelieving within the community.

- Teaching the people about an outward-focused God.

An outward-focused church must begin with building a solid theological foundation on God and the mission and work of Jesus Christ.

THE GREAT COMMISSION CULTURE

The "Great Commission Culture" is made up of three Great challenges: the Great Commission, to go; the Great Commandment, to love; and the Great empowerment that gives ability to accomplish the mission. In Scripture, Jesus clearly presented His purpose and involvement in these three challenges. And from beginning to end, the Bible communicates these principles in the lives of mankind, with the express plan that they will continue with every generation.

GREAT COMMISSION
GO

GREAT COMMANDMENT
LOVE

GREAT EMPOWERMENT
HOLY SPIRIT

Having a clear understanding of God's plan, helps leaders to ultimately focus the entire church on His purpose. The WHY of God's mission is wrapped up in all three principles combined. Spending time looking at the purpose of God's desired outward-focused church will help build a solid foundation for any church.

GREAT COMMISSION

The Old Testament starts with creation, from which point God has shown His desire for His creation to reach out and have fellowship with Him. That relationship was broken by Adam and Eve's sin in the Garden of Eden.

The court system uses the term *conciliation* when two parties are in need of a restored relationship. *Conciliation* requires one party taking a first step outside of the Court to bring peace and harmony into the center of a strife-filled relationship. This is often referred to as the *alternative dispute resolution,* where two parties bring their dispute to a third party.

The New Testament speaks of *conciliation* in terms of God's broken relationship with people. Prior to the cross, people were commanded by God to shed the blood of innocent animals as a covering for their sin. The blood of animals did not remove their sin but provided a temporary covering until

God could send a Conciliator. God chose to take the first step in this broken relationship by sending Jesus as the mediator to bring atonement for humanity (Romans 3:25; Hebrews 2:17; 1 John 2:2; 4:10). Before you were born, God took the first step of conciliation. Jesus took upon Himself your sin and shed His own blood to heal your broken relationship with God. Even in the midst of humankind's failure, this loving missionary God came up with a plan to send His only Son to bring reconciliation to a disconnected world.

In order for the broken relationship to be mended, reconciliation is needed. Reconciliation is man's response to God's conciliation. The price for reconciliation has been paid by Jesus, but until man recognizes his sin and calls out to Jesus, there can be no reconciliation with God.

God calls His church to be co-conciliators with Him. We are to be those who will go and take the first step into restoring the broken relationship that people have with their Heavenly Father. God's desire to restore fellowship with His creation is intense and never-ending. Throughout the pages of the Old Testament, we see God calling individuals to move beyond the status quo, to GO and be a blessing to the world, bringing the gospel of Jesus Christ.

The theology of an outward-focused conciliatory ministry begins in Scripture with God creating the garden of Eden for Adam and Eve to live in and cultivate. From the beginning, God made it clear that Eden was not the final location that He had intended for humankind. Before the Fall, God said to Adam and Eve, "Be fruitful and increase in number, fill the earth and subdue it."[13] God intended for Adam and Eve and their offspring to populate the entire earth.

Historically, people tend to colonize under groupings of language, geography, culture, and religion. Colonizing brings many comforts as communities benefit by the skills and labors of others.

There are many benefits that come with living in community: however, the church can fall into the temptation to colonize with an attitude of "Us only and no more."

God commanded humankind to go and fill the world. He intended for us to move from a settling inclination to a sending inclination and inhabit the earth.

The Bible records the account where the majority of the world's population ended up colonized in Babel (Genesis 11). Rather than following God's command to multiply and fill the earth, humankind chose to inhabit one city and build one culture. People have a tendency to nest, enjoying the accumulations of wealth for selfishness (Gen. 11:1-9):

> Their desire to "make a name" for themselves was opposed to the reign of God. The judgment that followed included the scattering of the peoples throughout the earth. This set the stage for the great declaration of Genesis 12:3 that through Abraham "all peoples" ("nations," TEV) would be blessed.[14]

God used situations like the Tower of Babel to disperse colonized people and send them around the world. In both the Babel account and the Upper Room account, found in Acts chapter two, He used the human tongue as a means to disperse people.

The first encounter at Babel came as a result of God's judgment on humanity's pride. Rather than following His command to multiply and fill the earth, people of the time chose to inhabit one city and build one culture. As a result of their rebellion, all of the residents received different languages from God. This experience served to form new groups of people, with different languages and cultures, who set out to populate the world.

The second experience came to the Jewish believers in Acts chapter two, as they were obeying Jesus command to wait for the empowerment of the Holy Spirit. God chose to use tongues again. However, this time, the new tongues received in the upper room were not forced or given out of judgment. They were given by the grace of God to the Jewish believers as a sign of the empowerment of the Holy Spirit. This empowerment enabled them to disperse from Jerusalem and begin sharing the good news, through the leading of the Holy Spirit, to all people groups inhabiting the world.

Throughout Scripture, we find God assuring individuals that He will go with them and bless them if they will leave the comforts of home, and instead journey to connect with people groups of different languages and cultures.

Noah, Abraham, and the Patriarchs, were called by God to go and speak relentlessly of His desire to bless and restore relationship with the inhabitants of the world. Then the time in history arrived when the perfect sacrifice was made, the price for all sin was paid, and the door was opened for restoration through Jesus Christ. Yes, Jesus came to earth "to seek and to save the lost" (Luke 19:10). Before He ascended to Heaven, He called His followers to love Him with complete love and obedience and to love their neighbors as themselves. In other words, to be co-conciliators with Him, bringing the hope of reconciliation throughout the world.

GOD IS A MISSIONARY GOD TO THIS CULTURE AND HIS CHURCH MUST TAKE A MISSIONARY POSTURE.

God's desire for fellowship with every person is intense. He chose to send His son to earth to become one hundred percent human (Romans 5:10; 2 Corinthians 5:21). As we begin to grasp the love and sacrifice God made for us, one of the first verses we learn in our Christian walk is John 3:16. However, that message was never meant to remain solely a personal promise. Our outward-focused God desires that all receive this message. When looking at the teachings of Jesus, one sees Him teaching His disciples to be outward-focused. He did not present the church with a menu from which they could choose what they wanted to leave off the plate. He issued a clear and succinct command, "to make disciples." He also called for the disciples to baptize these individuals, indicating that Jesus called these new followers to then go out into the world and continually make new disciples.

As we rise to the challenge to be more like Jesus, we will take His focus on reaching out to our world and become missionary-minded with churches that are outward-focused.

Another way to accept this challenging lifestyle is to look even closer at Jesus' teachings on the Kingdom of God. This topic was at the core of His conversations and mission, so it is important to take time to study that motif. The Kingdom of God was a major emphasis that can be traced back to traditions of the Old Testament. Then Jesus represented the good news concerning the Kingdom of God in His life and teachings. Jesus said to them, "I must proclaim the good news of the kingdom of God to the other towns also, because that is why I was sent" (Luke 4:43).

Instead of challenging the political or military systems of our world, Jesus used miraculous signs and wonders to present a Kingdom that ministers to the poor, weak, sick, hungry, oppressed, and underprivileged. He demonstrated a Kingdom that was both "now" and "not yet" by teaching that we should pray with the phrase "Your Kingdom come." He acted on the spiritual and earthly needs of people and changed their culture and environment. He desired the Church to carry on this focus of entering the Kingdom of God through faith and repentance. "The time has come," He said. "The kingdom of God has come near. Repent and believe the good news!" (Mark 1:15).

GREAT COMMANDMENT

The Great Commission, found in Matthew 28:16-20, is our call to GO and take this message of reconciliation to others.

I grew up in church. In fact, while growing up, my dad was my pastor. I always saw the Great Commission as something that foreign missionaries accomplished. My job was to put some money in the offering each month to help them carry out the Great Commission.

While in my mid-twenties, I re-launched a church in East Wenatchee, Washington. I soon discovered that planting a church was difficult. People would visit once and never show up again. We began supporting missionaries, but the church didn't grow. Why was the Great Commission not working? Could it be that I lacked the right focus?

It was around this time that I learned the impetus behind the command, not suggestion, of the Great Commission. And that impetus is that which we refer to as the Great Commandment.

> Then the eleven disciples went to Galilee, to the mountain where Jesus had told them to go. [17]When they saw him, they worshiped him; but some doubted. [18]Then Jesus came to them and said, "All authority in heaven and on earth has been given to me. [19]Therefore go and make disciples of all nations, baptizing them in the name of the Father and of the Son and of the Holy Spirit, [20]and teaching them to obey everything I have commanded you. And surely I am with you always, to the very end of the age." (Matthew 28:16-20)

In my second year as lead pastor, I received a call from a pastor friend of a large sister church in the Wenatchee Valley. The pastor sensed that I needed help. He invited me to join his church to attend a pastors' seminar at Phoenix First Assembly with pastor Tommy Barnett. I was reluctant to go because of the cost, but he explained his church was graciously picking up my travel, food, and lodging expense, so I could attend.

My theology was challenged the first night of the conference. I began to hear the heart of a pastor as Pastor Barnett read about the great banquet in Luke 14. In this story, the master told his servant to go out an invite everyone to the banquet. When the servant returned, he gave a negative report. Everyone he invited had an excuse for not attending. I immediately thought, "He has the same problem I have."

The master didn't let his servant off the hook easily. He told the servant to go out into the highways and the bi-ways and compel the unlovely to come in. The servant obeyed and the banquet was filled to overflowing.

Pastor Barnett began to invite the various outward-focused ministries of the church to the platform and interview those involved. I began to cry while hearing stories of changed lives; children reached through the bus ministry, former drug addicts, former prostitutes, and individuals with handicaps. They shared stories of being transformed through the love and grace of Jesus Christ. That night, I told the Lord that I would quit trying to do ministry my way. I would go back and obey the Great Commission by first following the Great Commandment.

The Great Commandment is our call to LOVE; fueling the work of the Great Commission with that love. The process of love was started by God in His missionary plan to love humankind back into relationship with Him.

> For God so loved the world that he gave his only Son that whoever believes in him shall not perish but have eternal life. For God did not send his son into the world to condemn the world, but to save the world through him (John 3:14-17).

I John 4:9-11 continues with this topic of God's love:

> This is how God showed his love among us: He sent his one and only son into the world that we might live through him. This is love: not that we loved God, but that he loved us and sent his Son as an atoning sacrifice for our sins. Dear friends, since God loved us, we also ought to love one another.

These verses declare that God is an outward-focused God who demonstrates His love for humankind. Love serves as a motivating factor for God who unselfishly sent Jesus. These scriptures reveal that God, being love, is on an outward-focused mission to redeem humankind.

The God of the Bible is a missionary God. Since the fall of the human race, God seeks to bring people back to Himself. God blessed Abraham and his descendants so that the world through them would be blessed. God's expectation was for

Israel to be a light to the Gentiles, and He condemned the nation when it failed in this mission (Isa 49:6, Rom. 10:18-21). So God provided redemption for the world through the Lord Jesus Christ. While Jesus was on earth, He stated that He would build His church and the gates of hell would not prevail against it. Later, the Apostle Paul taught that God displayed His wisdom by bringing both the Jews and Gentiles together as they both exercised faith in Jesus Christ to become part of this new entity called the Church.

GOD'S LOVE IS NOT A PASSIVE TYPE OF LOVE, LEAVING HUMANKIND TO SOLVE THEIR OWN DILEMMAS; IT REQUIRES OUTWARD-FOCUSED ACTION.

God has always had the positive purpose of love toward humankind. He isn't seeking a way to condemn, but rather a way to save. His very purpose in sending His Son into the world was to show humankind His love and draw them to Himself. The ability to love God stems from the understanding that He first loved us (I John 1:9). God is interested in a love relationship that is not one-sided. He continues to call us to love Him.

In Luke 10:25, a legal expert with a desire to test Jesus asks, "What must I do to inherit eternal life?" Jesus immediately turns the question around: "What is written in the law? How do you read it?" (Luke 10:26). The man responds by saying, "Love the Lord your God with all your heart and with all your soul and with all your strength and with all your mind; and, Love your neighbor as yourself" (Luke 10:27). Jesus replies, "You have answered correctly, do this and you will live." The expert continues to probe, asking, "*And who is my neighbor?*"

The term *Missio Dei* (Mission of God) begins with loving God with all of one's heart, soul, mind, and strength. The greatest commandment is to love the one true God exclusively from all other so-called gods. We must examine these commands to see the bigger plan of this missionary-God. The entire Word of God, and God's mission for humankind, rests on these two commandments.

WHO IS MY NEIGHBOR?

We cannot stop with simply loving God. Jesus declared that the second command is equally important, calling human-kind to love their neighbors as themselves. Jesus demon-strated this through His own lifestyle on earth. He loved His neighbors by His friendship with tax collectors and sinners. In Luke 10:27, Jesus agreed with the lawyer's answer and challenged him to live this way. The man then asked, "Who is my neighbor?" I believe this is the question that every Christ follower needs to ask of Jesus.

Jesus brought clarity to the fact that humans exist on earth for more reasons than receiving eternal life. They are called to love others as themselves. To love a neighbor as oneself does not mean to love them as much as you love yourself, but it does mean to love them in the way you would love yourself. Jesus illustrated this truth by telling the parable of the good Samaritan.

> *A man was going down from Jerusalem to Jericho, when he was attacked by robbers. They stripped him of his clothes, beat him and went away, leaving him half dead. A priest happened to be going down the same road, and when he saw the man, he passed by on the other side. So too, a Levite, when he came to the place and saw him, passed by on the other side. But a Samaritan, as he trav-eled, came where the man was; and when he saw him, he took pity on him. He went to him and bandaged his wounds, pouring on oil and wine. Then he put the man on his own donkey, brought him to an inn and took care of him. The next day he took out two denarii and gave them to the innkeeper. "Look after him," he said, "and when I return, I will reimburse you for any extra expense you may have." Which of these three do you think was a neighbor to the man who fell into the hands of robbers? The expert in the law replied, "The one who had mercy on him." Jesus told him, "Go and do likewise" (Luke 10:30-37).*

The legal expert asked Jesus a practical question, "Who is my neighbor?" Jesus' answer was the parable. The Samari-tan viewed the man as his neighbor. So we have to ask ourselves the question, "Am I behaving as a neighbor to those who need my love and help?" If not for the Samaritan, one despised by the Jewish community, the wounded man probably would have died. The Samaritan's concern for the man translated into sacrificial action. The Samaritan cleaned and bandaged his wounds, laid him on his donkey, and found him a room at the inn. He also provided for any services the man might need. The Samaritan demonstrated love through his actions.

Through this parable, Jesus articulated how people should love their neighbors as themselves. This outward-focused demonstration of care and concern turned a Samaritan into a neighbor. Jesus challenged the expert in the Law to go and do the same. If the lawyer loved God, he would go and love his neighbors in need of help. He would love his neighbor as he loved himself.

God, who is outward-focused, sends every believer into the world to respond to the Great Commission and the Great Commandment. To accomplish this outward-focused mission, we then need the empowerment that He has provided.

GREAT EMPOWERMENT

The doctrine of the baptism of the Holy Spirit has led to many differing opinions over the last 100 years. In the early 1900's, an impetus came out of Azusa Street, Los Angeles on evangelizing the World with the emphasis of the baptism of the Holy Spirit. These early Pentecostal believers depended on the empowerment of the Holy Spirit for witness as they came face to face with demonic powers.

During my lifetime, I have watched the Church reduce the importance of the baptism of the Holy Spirit to an inward-focused practice. Sermons on the Holy Spirit often cater to the consumer mindset of what the Spirit can do for the individual rather than emphasizing the primary purpose of empowerment for witness. The manifestations of the

Holy Spirit are often viewed as a practice that takes place only inside the church on Sunday mornings. We tend to be more concerned about what the Holy Spirit can do for *me*, rather than asking how the Holy Spirit can empower us for witness.

When studying the book of Acts, Jesus gives the "WHY" believers should desire the empowerment that He offers in Acts. "And you shall receive power, after the Holy Spirit comes upon you to be witnesses in Jerusalem, Judea, Samaria and the Uttermost parts of the Earth" (Acts 1:8). The power of the Holy Spirit was given for the purpose of taking the gifts of the Spirit to the marketplaces of the world. Jesus knew the Church would need the empowerment of the Holy Spirit to accomplish the call of witnessing to all the inhabitants of the earth.

Jesus modeled Spirit empowerment. Following the testing of Satan in the wilderness, Jesus, who was full of the Holy Spirit, left to return to Galilee. He entered the synagogue at Nazareth, opened the scroll to Isaiah 61, and read:

> *The Spirit of the Lord is on me,*
> *Because he has anointed me*
> *To proclaim good news to the poor,*
> *He has sent me to proclaim freedom for the prisoners*
> *And recovery of sight for the blind,*
> *to set the oppressed free,*
> *to proclaim the year of the Lord's favor*
> *(Luke 4:18-19).*

God was not trying to create Christians who would just survive until they entered heaven. Jesus knew that His followers would need Supernatural help from the Holy Spirit, just as He did, to accomplish the task of proclaiming good news and freedom to those in bondage.

In fact, Jesus wanted to reassure His followers they would not be doing this alone. These followers who responded to His call, even though some were struggling with doubts, heard Him say:

All authority in heaven and on earth has been given to me. Therefore, go and make disciples of all nations, baptizing them in the name of the Father and of the Son and of the Holy Spirit, and teaching them to obey everything I have commanded you. And surely I am with you always, to the very end of the age (Matthew 28:18-20).

During Jesus' final hours on earth, before His ascension, He spoke openly with words of reassurance to the believers. Combined with this great task before them was a promise of the power needed in their lives:

Then he opened their minds so they could understand the Scriptures. He told them, "This is what is written: The Messiah will suffer and rise from the dead on the third day, and repentance for the forgiveness of sins will be preached in his name to all nations, beginning at Jerusalem. You are witnesses of these things. I am going to send you what my Father has promised; but stay in the city until you have been clothed with power from on high (Luke 24:45-49).

The power that anointed Jesus for earthly ministry was the same power promised to His church, and delivered, on the day of Pentecost. The Holy Spirit empowered the disciples of Christ to carry on the works of Jesus and do even greater things than He did (John 14:12). This demonstration of power was different from that exhibited by the Roman government who ruled with force and fear. God's people, who were transformed by their love for God and their love for their neighbor, were empowered with a boldness to bring about a spiritual and cultural transformation to the regions in which they ministered. 1 John 4:19 tells us that because God loves us first, we then love Him in return. We demonstrate our love for Him through worship, prayer, praise, and service, as we love our neighbor as ourselves. He has given us the empowerment to bring the salvation message to a lost world.

THE BOOK OF ACTS PRESENTS AN INCREDIBLE PENTECOSTAL NARRATIVE CONCERNING THE KINGDOM OF GOD.

Ongoing records throughout the book of Acts show us the expansion of the Gospel message, the spread of the Church, and many examples of the change in lives as a result. Since the focus of a leader affects the focus of the church, let's look for a moment at how God changed the hearts of some early church leaders to create outward-focused individuals. Their new outlook not only gives us a personal testimony, but it also points to how God formed a Church that caught the importance of being outward-focused.

THE FOCUS OF A LEADER AFFECTS THE FOCUS OF THE CHURCH.

The book of Acts is filled with New Testament examples of outward-focused leaders. Two men in particular are the Apostles Paul and Peter. As you read about them below, consider how God may be expanding your own outward-focus.

The narrative in Acts begins with a Saul of Tarsus, who upon conversion, is then called the Apostle Paul. This man was then credited with the initial expansion of the gospel to both Jews and Gentiles. Paul lived in Jerusalem, studied under Gamaliel, a famous rabbinical teacher of that day, and had been influenced by many cultures in that Greco-Roman society. We pick up his life story at his miraculous conversion on the road to Damascus, where he received the call to God's mission. Paul's earlier training and lifestyle gave him an advantage for reaching beyond his own religious circle to connect with others outside the faith. Paul learned the relational skill of adaptation.

Paul's life in a multicultural society prepared him well to adapt and adjust. He was aware of the need to adapt his conduct and style of speech to fit his circumstances. He could deal with religious experts or converse with tentmakers. Although he was a Jew, he wrote in Greek and developed relationships with Gentiles. He was born with Hebrew parents, raised as a Roman citizen, and able to fully function in both the Hebrew and Roman cultures.

For the Church to successfully reach a multicultural world,

it must respond with adaptability in relational skills. A cross-cultural missionary understands that they must first learn the culture of the people they are called to reach. This means they spend time with them, learn their language, and begin to build relationships within that cultural setting. The Church often struggles with adaptability and resists looking through the lens of other people. Yes, Paul clearly warns about not allowing outsiders to weaken the message or purpose of the Church, but he balances that with the need to reach those who need Jesus.

Within that tension, Paul emphasized the importance of reaching all kinds of people with the Good News. "To those not having the law I became like one not having the law, (though I am not free from God's law but am under Christ's law) so as to win those not having the law" (1 Corinthians 9:20). He adapted to the needs of the people he wanted to reach. Paul kept the motivation of the Gospel, God's initiative for the salvation of humankind, as his focal point.

> For I am not ashamed of the gospel, because it is the power of God that brings salvation to everyone who believes: first to the Jew, then to the Gentile. The Gospel reveals God's righteousness–a righteousness by faith from beginning to end, just as it is written: "The righteous will live by faith" (Rom. 1:16-17).

Although adapting to a multicultural world, Paul kept a solid focus on the message of the outward-focused Church he was planting.

Like Paul, Peter came to realize the importance of an outward-focused ministry. We read the account of Peter, originally known as Simon, a married fisherman, brought to Christ by his brother Andrew. Peter's life and growth as a follower of Jesus are key elements in the gospels, and then he plays a dynamic leadership role as a missionary and pillar of the Church, as mentioned in Paul's writings (1 Cor. 9:5; Gal. 2:9). We capture this change in Peter on the day of Pentecost as recorded in the book of Acts.

> When the day of Pentecost came, Jewish believers gath-

ered together in an upper room in Jerusalem. Suddenly a sound like the blowing of a violent wind came from heaven and filled the whole house where they were sitting. They saw what seemed to be tongues of fire that separated and came to rest on each of them. All of them were filled with the Holy Spirit and began to speak in other tongues as the Spirit enabled them.

There were God-fearing Jews staying in Jerusalem from many nations of the world. When they heard this sound coming from the upper room, they came together in bewilderment, as each of them heard their own language. They asked each other: "Are not these men who are speaking Galileans? Then how is it that each of us hears them in his own native language? Parthians, Medes and Elamites; residents of Mesopotamia, Judea and Cappadocia, Pontus and Asia, Phrygia and Pamphilia, Egypt and parts of Libya near Cyrene; visitors from Rome (both Jews and converts to Judaism); Cretans and Arabs–we hear them declaring the wonders of God in our own tongues!"

Amazed and perplexed, they were asking one another, "What does this mean?" Some, however, made fun of them and said, "they have had too much wine" (Acts 2:1-13).

After reading this account, we can also note the powerful missionary account recorded in Acts 10 as Peter again received divine help and empowerment to reach the Gentiles. Peter's life and ministry was a living example of the fulfillment of Jesus' promise that the Holy Spirit's power would come upon believers, making them His "witnesses in Jerusalem, and in all Judea and Samaria, and to the ends of the earth" (Acts 1:8).

It had only been fifty days earlier that Peter had denied knowing Jesus. But on the Day of Pentecost, a new leader stepped up, empowered by the Holy Spirit, and ready to speak to a crowd from many cultures. Peter stood and addressed the multicultural Jewish crowd with boldness, calling them to "repent and be baptized in the name of Jesus Christ for the forgiveness of sins and to receive the gift of the Holy Spirit" (Acts 2:38). On that day, three thousand new converts were added to the present community of believers. The Church received power to witness about Christ, the Messiah, who died, was buried, and rose again.

The Apostle Peter is often viewed as the Father of the Early Church in Jerusalem. Acts 10 provides an impressive narrative of Peter's outward-focused journey, presenting God's interaction with two separate individuals during the same time frame: first, a Centurion named Cornelius, and second, Simon, an apostle living in Joppa, a city inhabited primarily by Jews.

During this time, Luke, the writer of Acts, begins with describing Cornelius, a Gentile, living in the city of Caesarea. Caesarea was from A.D. 6, the provincial capital and place of residence of the Roman governor. The Jews hated the Gentiles and the Roman Army, which served as a symbol of world power and had a stronghold on the Jews. However, Luke reveals Cornelius, a captain of the army, as one seeking after God: "He and all his family were devout and God-fearing; he gave generously to those in need and prayed to God regularly" (Acts 10:1-3).

While a good man and a seeker, Cornelius lacked one thing: salvation through Jesus Christ. God is always on the lookout for seekers. In this situation, He sent an angel down with a message for Cornelius: "Your prayers and your alms have come up for a memorial before God. Now send men to Joppa, and send for Simon whose surname is Peter. He is lodging with Simon, a tanner, whose house is by the sea. He will tell you what you must do" (Acts 10:4-6). Cornelius didn't waste time in searching for Peter. He quickly sent two of his servants to Joppa for Peter.

A day later, Peter saw a vision as God began to prepare his heart to overcome the prejudices that a Jewish man would have had about other nationalities. Peter had to learn the outward-focused concept of the Gospel for all people, not just the Jews. God used a sheet, unclean animals, and then His explanation to reveal "What God has cleansed, do not call common" (Acts 10:15).

For Peter, a Jew who always adhered to the Jewish dietary laws, this was a puzzling lesson. However, the lesson was quickly followed by the visit of three men.

> *Peter was directed to go downstairs and meet these men, and he soon understood the lesson God had for him. Simon went down the stairs, approached the men, saying, "I'm the one you're looking for. Why have you come?" The men replied, "We have come from Cornelius the centurion. He is a righteous and God-fearing man, who is respected by all the Jewish people. A holy angel told him to ask you to come to his house so that he could hear what you have to say." Then Peter invited the men into the house to be his guests (Acts 10:21-23).*

Peter's vision started to make sense to him. The three men invited Peter to travel with them to meet Cornelius as God had instructed (Acts 10:24).

The next day, the men travel with Peter to Caesarea. As Peter approached Joppa, Cornelius ran to meet him, falling down before him in worship. Peter grabbed him, explaining, "Stand up, I am just a man. The servant of God does not take glory for himself, but gives it to the Lord" (Acts 10:26). Peter continued, telling Cornelius, "You know how unlawful it is for a Jewish man to keep company with or go to one of another nation. But God has shown me that I should not call any man common or unclean" (v. 28).

Peter wasted no time articulating his faith. He told Cornelius about Jesus' birth, life, death, and resurrection, as well as the salvation available to Cornelius and everyone present. While Peter spoke, the Holy Spirit fell upon everyone, and Peter shares his new revelation and understanding of God's mission. Peter began to realize that God does not show favoritism toward nationalities but accepts anyone who fears Him and does what is right (Acts 10:34). As Peter was speaking, the Holy Spirit filled all the Gentiles listening to the message. Hearing the Gentiles speak in tongues and offer praise to God, Peter was amazed at how the Holy Spirit came upon them, and he encouraged them to be baptized in water (Acts 10: 44-48).

Peter's experience changed his theology concerning who could experience salvation. As He moved with an outward-focused calling, the Church became an outward-focused force that began to reach Gentiles with the gospel of Jesus Christ.

THE MISSION OF THE CHURCH IS TO JOIN GOD IN HIS REDEMPTIVE WORK TO BRING SALVATION TO HUMANKIND.

The question needs to be asked: Does your theology reflect the heart of an outward-focused God? The next chapter is going to help us assess the focus of our ministry. Many leaders assume their focus is clear, when in reality they have experienced a gradual loss of focus.

VISION CHECK

1. Why does your church exist?

2. What can you do to accomplish the Luke 14 challenge?

3. How do you demonstrate love to others?

4. What difference does the power of the Holy Spirit make in your personal life?

5. Does your theology reflect the heart of an outward-focused God? Explain.

Chapter 3

EXAMINING YOUR FOCUS

E very system of your church or ministry must be examined through outward-focused lenses. There are numerous points to consider when comparing a "country club" mentality with a "missional community," as discussed in the opening chapter. Examining the systems deals with assessing your church to discover its focus.

DETERMINE THE DISCONNECT

When you visit the optometrist for a vision screening, he or she will check each eye, your collective vision, and your eyesight under various conditions. The doctor helps to find the disconnect in your vision and determines various strengths as well as any weaknesses. Some of us need help with distance vision or struggle with reading distances, others suffer diminished night vision or have issues with bright lighting.

Just as every person must assess what the strengths and weaknesses of their vision is, likewise, churches must take a comprehensive look at their strengths as well as assess what they need to improve. When determining our outward-focused vision, we need to assess the culture of our community, current membership, and our personal understanding of God's mission for us.

I suggest you pause and reflect on your current church or ministry and its values. Don't repeat what you have written somewhere as your church mission statement, but begin to formulate a list of things your church values. Let me give you some examples.

For many churches, the building has become very sacred. The style of the facility, its design, and even the furniture is important. Some other churches are known for their style of music. A rocking worship band, a symphonic orchestra, a robed choir, or coordinated worship team, can be highly valued by a church, leadership or the community. Other churches value their reputation for the pastor's preaching style: fiery, academic, friendly, simple, or flamboyant.

Most churches have artifacts or icons that can become sacred. Perhaps you have a pulpit, a picture, or even a room that was named in someone's honor. These are prized possessions and often represent meaningful milestones or significant members in the church's history. What artifacts or icons in your church are people saying should never change?

The next challenge is to prayerfully list how these unstated church values hinder an outward-focus. If you really take the time to do this exercise, you will begin to see the disconnect between them and your desire to be an outward-focused church. The question is, *do you value your current style and facility more than the needs of your community?*

ACCESS THE NEEDS

The next obvious step is to assess the real needs of your community.

The community to consider is the area where your ministry takes place. If you live in a rural area, this could mean the entire town, but in most places it refers to a radius around your place of ministry.

Recently, two churches were planning outreach events in their communities. Both exist within the same zip code, but they are located at opposite ends of the city. The one congregation planned a food and clothing drive to help desperate families with low incomes. They planned events and began the process of a successful church plant with morning groups and afternoon activities.

The second church existed in a well established suburban neighborhood. Morning and afternoon outreaches were launched to reach children but failed because homes were empty while parents were at work and kids stayed in school. Community Assessment is vital before launching events or planting churches. The key to assessment is discovering the actual needs of the community.

Think about the community in which you serve. Understanding the demographic of your neighborhood is important to meeting the needs of the community. There is a big difference between the need for food items and the need for reasonable childcare for working adults. The needs you discover will affect your strategy and ministries.

The good news of the Gospel is for everyone, but the way it is presented needs to be focused on your community. Assessing the community will reveal how you can meet the needs of those living there. Church is not about people meeting the needs of the church, but the church learning how to meet the needs of the community. If you want to see your community change, it starts with a clear picture of the people who live there.

COMMUNITY TRANSFORMATION WILL NEVER HAPPEN WITHOUT A SINCERE COMPASSION FOR PEOPLE.

Recalling the Good Samaritan example from the Bible, we know we are to minister to the needs of our neighbor, but that requires compassion.

THE DECISION FOR COMPASSION

The choice to use compassion ministries can be a difficult one for some churches and even some denominations. For many years, evangelical churches would label churches involved in compassion ministries as presenting a social gospel.

A debate on this subject surfaced with the Assemblies of God during the 2009 Orlando Florida General Council meetings. A resolution was presented to the assembly expressing a desire to add the term 'compassion' as the Assemblies of God's fourth purpose for existing. The purpose statement would then read evangelism, worship, discipleship, and compassion.[14]

The resolution was at first defeated. Following the vote, George Wood commented on the resolution's defeat by writing, "I determined in the early morning hours of Friday, August 7, that I was going to yield the chair during the next business session, go to the floor, and appeal to the delegates to reconsider Thursday's action and adopt the resolution. One of the most satisfying moments in my life came when the delegates did just that."[15]

In my opinion, many of the opposing comments were presented by members who did not have a clear understanding of the Kingdom of God and His mission. Some thought the resolution would dilute the Fellowship's resolve to provide "the greatest evangelism the world has ever seen."[16] Others expressed concern that the movement would result in the Assemblies of God adopting a "social gospel" becoming like other mainline denominations that had navigated away from the truth of the Gospel message. Richard Schoonover, the associate editor for Enrichment journal wrote, "Compassion ministry is more than handing out groceries and clothing, cleaning up your community, or working hand-in-hand with community organizations. Compassion ministry is loving people just as God through Christ loves them (Psalm 146:7-9)."[17]

Your ministry must determine how to best demonstrate true compassion for the community you want to reach. That requires time spent assessing your community and its needs. An affective assessment consists of two vital areas. First, assessment of the community you live in and second, assessment of the present culture of your church.

THE DISCOVERY

To begin the discovery process, one must start by assessment of your community. When it comes to changing culture, the church can learn from secular corporations. Over the last decade, a great deal of research about culture exists. Successful secular organizations spend millions of dollars in research concerning culture that exists in your communities.

DEMOGRAPHIC ASSESSMENT

The first step in determining the demographics of your community begins with a fresh look outside your church building. When was the last time you simply walked around the neighborhood? Take a short drive of a few miles radius and look at the homes and businesses there. What is the landscape like in the mornings, afternoons, and evenings? Are there primarily families with kids playing or senior adults? Is this a place where many homeless are seen, or do the streets seem empty during working hours? Can you determine the average income level by the style of homes, vehicles, and clothing? There are many other factors to assess, but first it is important to observe your neighborhood.

Another way to assess your community is to check on the current status of the local schools, medical centers, and businesses. Friendly conversations with local business people, school administrators, and community leaders will often clarify what others perceive as the needs of your community. There are also internet sites that help with community information.

The Northwest Ministry Network provides demographics assessments free of charge to Network churches through MissionInsite, an organization that provides the most up to date statistics for church demographics. Each church can allow up to twenty people to log on to MissionInsite and conduct demographic assessment of their communities. A new Quadrennium report provides local community data concerning beliefs about God, Jesus, and social and moral issues. The survey also provides information of religious affiliations and preferences of the community. [18]

MULTI-CULTURAL ASSESSMENT

Many Anglo churches are living in a fog, thinking that the complexion of our nation has not changed over the last 30 years and neither have many of its methods and organizational structures. A new appreciation for diversity will be needed if the church is going to make this cultural shift. To often, the church thinks of people groups as races versus varying cultures. As long as we think in terms of race, we will assign stereotypes upon individuals on the basis of physical characteristics and generalizations. The church as a whole tends to have the philosophy that these groups are better off in creating their own churches and groups. In some respects, that might be true, but many times, it is an avoidance of the cultural integration challenges.

In the Assemblies of God, most of the multicultural churches are organized by way of language. The challenge with language-based churches happens when these individuals have children and grandchildren who are born in America and attend public school, dress like everyone else, and desire to speak English over their mother language. New innovative changes will need to take place in both the business world and the church as Western European Americans move towards becoming the minority in the United States.

CHURCH CULTURAL ASSESSMENT

Another avenue in discovering your community is to help your members identify what they believe to be the needs of others. Ask those within the church to talk about the needs of their co-workers, neighbors, friends, and relatives. Let them evaluate the schools, clubs, and government in your area, and see how they perceive the poor and needy. Some will be able to articulate the needs of those in the community while others will struggle.

Many established churches began in a part of town that is very different today. The original members may have moved farther away from the church's location, and they are not really connected to the community where the church building exists. An example would be those who now live in a distant suburb and no longer connect with the inner city needs near the church, or those who live in rural communities who drive in from farms or ranches and fail to really connect with the townsfolk living around the church. During this part of the assessment process, you may be most surprised by the lack of perception, connection, or tolerance by church members looking at their community. These are huge signals that you may have a very inward-focused church that simply doesn't see the need for being outward-focused.

Now you are beginning to capture the idea of how inward-focused you may have become and the shifts you will need to make in redirecting your ministry to be outward-focused.

This examination process is necessary to check your ministry vision. In the next chapter, I will guide you in a cultural transition process of refocusing your ministry.

VISION CHECK

1. What are the present needs in your community?

2. Are any churches or organizations presently minister-
    ing to the needs of the community?

3. What compassion ministries does your church cur-
    rently provide?

4. How would you define the neighborhood where your
    church is located?

5. Which forms of assessment do you still believe need
    to be done to better understand your neighborhood?

Chapter 4
ADJUSTING FOCUS

A young pastor attended a seminar that encouraged re-modeling the auditorium to enhance the worship experience. He returned home to his church and quickly began to design plans of re-purposing the seventy year old "sanctuary" painted white with its laminated beams and large cross that hung over the baptistery directly behind the pulpit. Plans included painting the front of the church black, adding stage lights and fog machines and theatre chairs. The young pastor brought these ideas to the church board meeting with great excitement. Immediately following his presentation, the new ideas were quickly squelched as other leaders explained that it could not be done, it wouldn't work, and it had never been done that way before. The tenured leaders made it very clear that the "sanctuary" was to remain a place of worship and not a concert hall.

The pastor left feeling like the board members were against his leadership and contemplated resigning on the spot. He had failed to take into consideration what the cultural values and attitudes were of the seventy year old congregation. When he began to mess with the artifacts, he immediately received a negative reaction.

Any time you get a reaction from the members when you want to change, you are bumping up against existing culture.

Edgar Schein in his book, *Organizational Culture and Leadership*, provides an excellent framework for understanding and assessing culture and leadership within an organization. Schein challenges the reader to learn to see the organization through cultural lenses, to a point where one can be more competent in cultural analysis and change.[19]

THREE MAJOR LEVELS FOR CULTURAL ANALYSIS:

- ARTIFACTS

- ESPOUSED BELIEFS AND VALUES

-UNDERLYING ASSUMPTIONS

To solve an inward-focused problem in the church, three basic aspects must be examined; artifacts, espoused beliefs and values, and underlying assumptions. The following model guides the leader to develop assessment and strategy for cultural change. As you read this chapter, consider how this could work in your setting.

THE BEGINNING STAGE

The beginning stage is all about asking the right questions. These outward-focused questions serve as one way to determine if the established church is living an outward-focused lifestyle and assist in defining what needs to change. Andy Stanley, pastor of Northpoint Community Church in Atlanta, Georgia, emphasizes the need for asking the right questions: "Asking the right questions (and asking them over and over) will ensure that the vision of your church remains paramount while your programming remains subservient."[20]

A SHARED CULTURAL ANALYSIS

Shared Cultural Analysis begins by asking your leadership teams the question, "What Problems do we want to solve?"

The essence of the assessment process is to bring together one or more representative groups in the organization, provide them a model of how to think about organizational culture and subcultures, and then ask them to identify the main artifacts, the espoused values, and the shared tacit assumptions, with an outsider playing the role of facilitator. A member of the organization in a leadership role can be the facilitator, as long as it is not his or her own department, and as long as he or she has an understanding of how culture works.

This kind of assessment is based on several key assumptions:

- Culture is a set of shared assumptions; hence, obtaining the initial data in a group setting is more appropriate and valid than conducting individual interviews.

- The contextual meaning of cultural assumptions can only be fully understood by members of the culture.

OBTAIN LEADERSHIP BUY-IN

Deciphering cultural assumptions and evaluating their relevance to some organizational change program must be viewed as a major intervention in the organization's life, and therefore, must only be undertaken with the full understanding and consent of the formal leaders of the organization.

SELECT GROUPS FOR SELF-ASSESSMENT

The next step is for the facilitator to work with the formal leaders to determine how best to select some groups representative of the corporate culture. The criteria for selection usually depend on the concrete nature of the problem to be solved. Groups can either be homogeneous, with respect to a given department, or groups can be rank level, or made deliberately heterogeneous, by selecting diagonal slices from the organization.

Inform the groups of the purpose of the meetings. There must be openness and candor.

CHOOSE AN APPROPRIATE SETTING FOR THE GROUP SELF-ASSESSMENT

The group meeting should stimulate perceptions, thoughts, and feelings that are ordinarily implicit. The room in which the meeting is to be held must therefore be comfortable, allow people to sit in a circular format, and permit the hanging of many sheets of flip chart paper on which cultural elements will be written.

CLARIFYING THE PURPOSE OF THE MEETING

The organizational change problem should be clearly stated and written down, allowing for questions and discussion. The purpose of this step is not only to be clear as to why this meeting is being held, but also to begin to get the group involved in the process. Note the time suggestions are added to the actual meeting steps to help you use time well and organize your presentation.

A SHORT SUMMARY ON HOW TO THINK ABOUT CULTURE

The Cultural Assessment Process is explained with a teaching on the difference between artifacts, assumptions, and attitudes. Time should be given to define the present mission of the church and clarify why the church exists.

THE PLATINUM CIRCLE

The Golden Circle, referred to in chapter 2, serves the leader well to look at the why, what, and how of ministry. However, it does not complete the entire implementation process.

In order to develop a complete model describing this process, I developed the platinum circle, adding two additional steps that include when the plan would be executed and who would be a part of this cultural transition. This stage is referred to as the implementation stage. The platinum circle will help the leader work through each step of the cultural change process.

THE PLATINUM CIRCLE

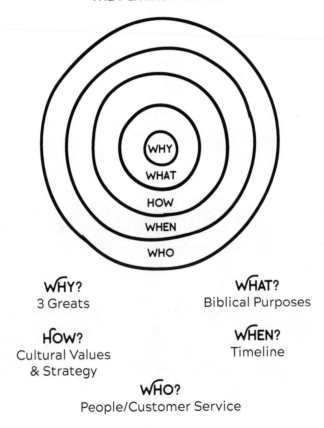

WHY?
3 Greats

WHAT?
Biblical Purposes

HOW?
Cultural Values
& Strategy

WHEN?
Timeline

WHO?
People/Customer Service

These steps begin from the center and move outward. They will help you to think through the issues, but the leader must work through the implementation process before change can take place. Look at the steps below to determine what is needed for cultural change.

5 STEPS TO CULTURAL CHANGE

STEPS 1-3: THE ASSESMENT STAGE

The purpose is to reach some kind of consensus on what the important shared assumptions are and their implications for what the organization wants to do.[22]

STEPS 4 &5: THE IMPLEMENTATION STAGE

These stages move out of the assessment stage into the action stage. They describe how and when the organization is going to bring execution of the values, artifacts, and assumptions.

STEP ONE - WHY

Why do we do what we do?
Goals: Define Mission

Step one is the starting point to cultural change. We must start with why we do what we do. Only once steps one through three are clearly defined and the problems have been discovered, can an organization move to the "WHEN" and "WHO" stage.

There is no easy short cut to move to stage four and five.

Steps one through three are necessary stages for cultural change. Cultural transformation is necessary; however, if an organization does not complete the "When" and "Who" stage, nothing further will transform.

A LEADER MUST BEGIN ASKING TWO QUESTIONS:
"HOW ARE WE DOING?"[21] AND "WHAT ARE WE DOING?"
AFTER ANSWERING THESE QUESTIONS, THE LEADER
OF AN ORGANIZATION MUST COURAGEOUSLY
FOLLOW THROUGH TO KEEP THE PEOPLE THEY LEAD
ACCOUNTABLE.

STEP TWO - WHAT
What are we doing?
Goals: Define Biblical Purposes

Having established the Why, the process consultant then tells the group that they are going to start by describing the culture through its artifacts. In other words: what are we doing currently? A useful way to begin is to find out who has joined the group most recently and ask that person what it felt like to enter the organization and what she or he noticed most upon entering it. Everything mentioned is written down on a flip chart, and as the pages are filled, they are torn off and hung on the wall so that everything remains visible.

Following are examples of cultural aspects that might get mentioned: dress codes, desired modes of behavior in addressing the boss, the physical layout of the sanctuary, how time and space are used, what kinds of emotions in others get noticed, how people get rewarded and punished, how someone gets ahead in the organization, how decisions are made, how conflicts and disagreements are handled, how work and family life are balanced, and so forth.

Apple Computer conducted some cultural assessments in the 1980s for the purpose of identifying how their rate of growth would impact their organizational structure and needs for physical expansion. On the list of artifacts, they noted that they spend a great deal of time in planning and in documenting the plans, but that the plans usually got overridden by the needs of a here-and-now crisis. They had put planning on their list of espoused values and felt genuinely puzzled and ashamed that they followed through so little on the plans they had made. This raised the whole issue of how time was perceived, and, after some discussion, the group members agreed that they operated from a deeper shared assumption that could best be stated as "Only the present counts." Once they stated the assumption in this form, they immediately saw on their own artifact list other items that confirmed this. They also thought of several new artifacts that further reinforced their orientation toward and preoccupation with the immediate present.

TIME SHOULD BE GIVEN TO ANSWER THE FOLLOWING QUESTIONS:[23]

1. What is going on here?
2. What are our Biblical Purposes?

BIBLICAL PURPOSES GIVE THE WHAT OF THE CHURCH.

Worship
to encounter Christ's presence
Hebrews 10:25

Instruction
to teach Christ followers
Acts 2:42

Fellowship
to encourage for Christ followers
1 Thessalonians 5:11; Hebrews 3:13

Service
to care for Christ followers
Galatians 6:2

Empowerment for Witness
to reach and have compassion for those
outside the church community
Romans 12:7; 1 Peter 4:10; 5:2-3 [24]

Avoiding any of these biblical purposes tends to contribute to an unhealthy and immature church. When a church correctly observes these purposes, it emerges healthy and outward-focused.

STEP THREE - HOW
How are we going to do it?
Goals: Define Values, Assumptions, Attitudes,
Strategies, and Systems

The next task is to categorize the assumptions according to whether they will aid or hinder the change process that is being pursued.

What are the attitudes or values of the present culture?

What assumptions are strengths and what are weaknesses?

What is not being said publicly but highly valued?

What are the strong reactions when you step on a core issue?

STEP FOUR - WHEN
When are we going to do it?
Goals: Execution

How aligned are the strategies and systems with your vision and values? In many cases, the ability to execute a plan serves as the difference between a successful company and its competitor. Many leaders delegate the skill of execution so they can spend time on the larger issues. Successful leaders must develop the discipline of execution. Leaders can come up with great strategies, but they will fail miserably if they cannot execute.

STEP FIVE - WHO
Who is going with us?
Goals: Execution

Step four requires asking the "WHEN" questions. When are we going to execute the plan? How aligned are the strategies and systems with our vision and values?

Step five involves getting the right people going the right direction at the right time. We must ask, who is going with us to accomplish the mission?

After these questions are answered, the leader of an organization must courageously follow through to keep the people they lead accountable.

A leader must be in charge of three basic processes: the ability to pick other leaders, setting the strategic direction, and conducting operations.[25]

The implementation stage is a necessary component to bringing about change in the organization's culture. Michael A. Beitler, in his book, *Strategic Organizational Change*, wrote, "Change is a process that follows a relatively predictable pattern."[26] Unfortunately, few pastors have received formal training about the change process.

When it comes to leading change, I recommend Kotter's eight step plan as one of the best guides for organizational change. Kotter's eight step plan includes steps two through nine of the list below.[27] These eight reasons (2-9) often are neglected and cause organizations to fall into complacency.[28]

1. Prayer.
2. Establish a sense of urgency.
3. Create a guiding coalition.
4. Develop vision and strategy for the specific change.
5. Communicate the change vision and strategic plan.
6. Empower employees for action.
7. Generate short-term wins.
8. Consolidate gains and produce more change.
9. Anchor the new changes in the culture.
10. Prayer.

Implementing prayer at the beginning and the end of the process is critical in any organizational change process. I recommend a 10 step plan to include prayer.

Cultural change takes place when this process is used repeatedly for any change initiative. Culture is often transformed over a period of time with incremental changes. When all eight steps are carried out with each change, the organization will own the change and the change will be anchored into the culture. Special care must be given to not skip any step in the process.

We will look at each of these steps as it relates to transitioning an inward-focused church into becoming an outward-focused church.

STEP ONE
PRAYER

C.S. Lewis once wrote, "God designed the human machine to run on Himself. He Himself is the fuel our spirits were designed to burn, or the food our spirits were designed to feed on. There is no other."[29]

When it comes to the church, everything must begin and end in prayer with Christ at the center of His Church. Jesus wants your church to grow even more than you want it to grow. He offers His creative ideas and the power of the Spirit to bring the ideas to reality.

STEP TWO
ESTABLISH A SENSE OF URGENCY

One of the greatest mistakes Pastors make when trying to change the culture, is to dive ahead without creating any discontent with the status-quo.

If a congregation is content with the status-quo, little

change will take place until they sense the urgency for change. The pain of staying the same will need to be greater that the pain of change before a congregation will choose to move beyond the status-quo.[30] I agree with Kotter's choice of placing this step as number one. If complacency is high, transformation will seldom take place and motivation will be low to solve the problem. Kotter states, "With urgency low, it's difficult to put together a group with enough power and credibility to guide the effort or to convince key individuals to spend the time necessary to create and communicate a change vision."[31]

REASONS FOR COMPLACENCY

CIRCLE ANY REASONS BELOW THAT YOU CAN IDENTIFY WITH YOUR CHURCH.

THE ABSENCE OF A MAJOR AND VISIBLE CRISIS

TOO MANY VISIBLE RESOURCES

LOW OVERALL PERFORMANCE STANDARDS

ORGANIZATIONAL STRUCTURES THAT FOCUS MEMBERS ON NARROW FUNCTIONAL GOALS

INTERNAL MEASUREMENT SYSTEMS THAT FOCUS ON THE WRONG PERFORMANCE INDEXES

A LACK OF SUFFICIENT PERFORMANCE FEEDBACK FROM EXTERNAL SOURCES

A KILL-THE-MESSENGER-OF-BAD-NEWS, LOW-CANDOR, LOW-CONFRONTATION CULTURE

HUMAN NATURE, WITH ITS CAPACITY FOR DENIAL, ESPECIALLY IF PEOPLE ARE ALREADY BUSY OR STRESSED

TOO MUCH HAPPY TALK FROM CHURCH LEADERSHIP

People will unconsciously reinforce the status-quo to protect complacency. When left to our own plans and void
of any compelling need for change, the status quo usually looks good. Church people tend to get inward-focused
with their friends. They can view outsiders as a threat to the
wonderful relationships that exist in the church.

MOST CHURCHES DO NOT BECOME
SMALL OVERNIGHT.

In fact, the plateauing and eventual decline generally oc-
cur when there is no visible or major crisis. Many visible
resources may exist from blessings of the past including
plush buildings with board rooms furnished with beautiful
mahogany tables. Performance standards erode over time
when staff focus on narrow functional goals. Many times the
lead Pastor becomes the one responsible for overall attendance and finances. As a result, a lack of measurement systems tend to focus on the wrong performances. More emphasis is placed on attendance and finance factors versus
the number of people baptized in water and introduced to
a discipleship ministry. Leadership can isolate themselves
from listening to the congregation and other performance
feedback loops that could reveal organizational blind spots.
In time, a culture exists where any person who communicates a negative word is viewed as an instigator and trouble
maker. Any messenger of bad news is viewed as a threat.
The organizational leaders would rather live in denial especially when stressed and filled with a busy routine. The culture then morphs into a happy talk culture where everything
is spun with a positive twist.

THIS TYPE OF COMPLACENT CULTURE MUST BE
CONFRONTED WITH A SENSE OF URGENCY. URGENCY
FOR THE CHURCH BEGINS WITH A GREAT COMMISSION
CULTURE THAT LEADS TO ACTION.

The church must be awakened to the truth that such complacency will ultimately keep many from the community of
God and the opportunity of knowing Jesus Christ. Kotter reveals, "Creating a strong sense of urgency usually demands

bold or even risky actions that we normally associate with good leadership."[32] These bold moves are needed to confront complacency in the church. Bold means a clear financial balance sheet that reveals a huge loss for the quarter. Bold may mean selling the church building that has accumulated a large debt that is suffocating the ministry. Bold means hiring outside coaches and consultants who deliver honest information at meetings, regardless of the people it may upset.

STEP THREE
CREATE A GUIDING COALITION

The day of the isolated CEO or pastor is over.

In today's fast changing world, no single individual is able to develop the right vision, eliminate all the challenges, and bring deep change to the organization's culture.[33] Pastors must establish cohesive teams that will help move the vision forward. Kotter recommends pulling together a team that has four characteristics.

First, they must have position power. Find enough board members so those who are left out cannot easily block progress. Second, find people with expertise in the various systems of the organization. Third, build a team that has credibility, so its announcements to the entire constituency are taken seriously. Fourth, find enough proven leaders who can help bring about the change process.[34]

STEP FOUR
DEVELOP A VISION AND STRATEGY
FOR THE SPECIFIC CHANGE

No leader should single-handedly develop the vision and strategy but must depend on the guiding coalition to be a part of the process.

The vision for this change must inspire the leaders of the organization through a shared vision.[35] The vision statement gives a picture into the future with some emphasis on why the people should believe in creating that future.[36]

STEP FIVE
COMMUNICATE THE CHANGE VISION
AND STRATEGIC PLAN

Next, everyone in the organization has to be working from the same vision and plan. So you must communicate that vision and plan.

Pastors easily make the mistake of thinking everyone has bought into the vision and plan. People prefer to be part of the change process rather than being told after the fact. The key in the process is to develop trust among the members. If trust is destroyed at this phase, forward momentum for change will be difficult. The boxed section on the next page shows Kotter's suggestions for effective communication.[37]

STEP SIX
EMPOWER EMPLOYEES AND VOLUNTEERS
FOR BROAD-BASED ACTION

Empowering employees is based on the leadership principle called path-goal theory.

Path-goal (perhaps, more accurately, goal-path) leadership style starts with establishing a goal with the employee. Then, the leader's remaining responsibility is to help clear the path so that the employee can accomplish the goal."[38] Leaders create barriers for employees if formal structures make it difficult to act, lack of skills or information undermine action, or the boss discourages actions for the employee to implement the new vision.

THE PASTOR'S STAFF MUST BE EMPOWERED AND ENCOURAGED TO HELP BRING ABOUT THE CHANGE PROCESS.

They need the best information at the time for making the best decisions possible. Empowerment of the staff may require a change in the leadership of the pastor. The command-and-control style of leadership must transition to a collaborative team approach that encourages empowerment of every staff member.[39]

EFFECTIVE COMMUNICATION OF THE VISION

Simplicity
Avoid jargon and technobabble

Analogy
Come up with a verbal picture

Multiple Forums
Communicate in big and small meetings, memos, tweets, texts, blogs and newsletters

Repetition
Ideas must be heard many times before they sink in

Leadership Example
Leadership behavior must be consistent with the vision communicated

Give-and-Take
Inconsistencies undermine the credibility of all communication

Explanation of Inconsistencies
Two-way communication is always better than one-way communication

---

STEP SEVEN
GENERATE SHORT-TERM WINS

This step cannot be ignored when attempting to change culture. There are many resisting forces working against change. A leader must aim those resisting forces toward the committed goal.

CELEBRATING SHORT WINS HELPS TO BUILD CREDIBILITY THROUGHOUT THE PROCESS.

When celebrating short term wins, Kotter lists three important characteristics of short-term wins. They are visible; they are unambiguous; and they clearly relate to the change agent.[40] Kotter presents a general rule: "The more cynics and resisters, the more important are short-term wins."[41] They key is to generate momentum while bringing about change.

STEP EIGHT
CONSOLIDATE GAINS AND
PRODUCE MORE CHANGE

During the transition, leaders must constantly monitor the progress of the change agent as resisting forces look for a way to return and find complacency.

Emphasis on the desired outcome is necessary to stay focused throughout the change process.[42] There may be times when a new plan must be adapted to build further support.

STEP NINE
ANCHOR THE NEW CHANGE
IN THE CULTURE

Once the organizational culture changes are made, leaders must work to make those changes part of the norms of behavior and shared values of the people.[43]

Kurt Lewin termed this step as "refreezing" in his model of cultural change.[44] Over time, new staff members and groups of people will strive to enhance their own self-interests. The greatest deterrent to change in a group is the culture. Once the norms and values of the group changes, the leader will know they have changed the culture. Kotter states, "Whenever you hear of a major restructuring, reengineering, or strategic redirection in which step one is "changing the culture." you should be concerned that it might be going down the wrong path."[45] When it comes to anchoring change, the reminders below provide important instruction.[46]

COMES LAST, NOT FIRST
Most alterations in norms and shared values come at the end of the change process

DEPENDS ON RESULTS
New approaches generally sink into culture after it is clear that they work

REQUIRES A LOT OF TALK
Without clear verbal communication and support, people are reluctant to change

MAY INVOLVE TURNOVER
Sometimes, when people are resistant to change, there must be a change in key people

MAKES DECISIONS ON SUCCESSION CRUCIAL
Promotion processes must change to be compatible with the new practices or the culture will reassert itself

STEP TEN
PRAYER

Be sure to anchor the change in prayer. You started in prayer, and now it is time to anchor the creative change process in prayer. Pray that Jesus will help your church become an outward-focused force in your community and the world. Pray that the church will continue to move outward as a united community while being on mission.

Do you want to have a thriving outward-focused church, moving away from the old inward-focused areas of ministry? This is no easy task, but it is possible with a clear process and with the help of God. Take a moment to refresh the goal behind this process: to reflect God's outward-focused love and to edify His mission of bringing that Good News to all people.

There will be times when the assessment and implementation gets tedious or difficult, yet this is an important part of our leadership in ministry. The next chapter will speak to what follows in this process. The work of His Kingdom is never completed, so you have probably already guessed that ongoing processes, specifically reassessing our focus, will always be necessary.

VISION CHECK

1. Which step will be the most difficult for your church in the Schein Model? Why?

2. Have you begun the implementation stage? How?

3. Which step of Kotter's plan for change will be the easiest for your church? Why?

4. In what areas of growth do you feel your church has become complacent?

5. Who do you see on your team who will help with change?

6. What areas of change will require a continued prayer focus?

Chapter 5

OUTWARD-FOCUSED LENSES

t's been about three years since the church was plant-ed. The church is gaining new families, ministries have fresh leadership, and the pastor has been preaching out-ward-focused messages. This year the church has noticed the new multi-story housing units a block away have been completed and tenants are starting to fill the area. Half of the new residents are from the 55 and above side and the other half are young families. A number of individuals 55 and older are now part of the church and desire the church to take care of their increasing needs and demands.

Whether you are a leader of a recent church plant or the leader of a mature existing church, re-assessment should take place on regular basis. Church planters often believe they are immune from inward-focused tendencies. How-ever, if the leader does not protect the outward-focused culture, inward-focused culture will take place within six months to a year. The group that started with you will of-ten transition out in time and the core will begin to demand certain rights of belonging.

An outward-focused church is a community on mission.

During the nineteenth and twentieth centuries, a new cul-tural accommodation arose. The church began to accom-modate privatism. Revivalists began to reduce the Chris-tian experience to personal conversion.[47] Consequently, the Church must now gain a larger worldview than individualism since God calls them into community on mission with Him.

God is calling the Church to His story; it involves commu-nities. His story includes governments in cities, counties, states, and nations. God chose to use Scripture to share His narrative with the world.[48] In the book *Servolution*, Dino Rizzo writes how the church can know it is making an im-pact: "We are learning that whenever you find something that meets a need and makes people excited about com-ing to church, it is probably worth doing."[49] A community on mission understands that God has placed them in the community to meet the basic needs of people.

An outward-focused church believes it can make a positive

96

difference in many people's lives.

Scripture reveals God called a community, a Spirit-empowered people, to witness the gospel in their context and create new faith communities (Eph. 4:1).[50] The call to Christ entails more than just a call to salvation–the beginning of the journey. It means a call to be a witness in all aspects of life and ministry. The Church's calling includes living as God's people in missional community.[51]

A church must ask the question, "What does a missional community look like, and how does a church transform its Ecclesiology?" Outward-focused is not so much about style as it is culture. Believers do not become outward-focused by merely meeting in a coffee house or homeschool group. An outward-focused culture happens with intentionality.

Annual eye exams are needed to keep our proper focus. In that same thought, leaders and ministries need to reassess their focus on a regular basis. The process started with evaluation and steps to determine the real vision of the church. Then the ongoing work of shifting from an inward-focused to an outward-focused mentality took time and a lot of effort. Much like our physical eyesight, once you correct the vision problem with glasses, you are not finished with the job. Annual eye exams are needed which usually result in new lenses to meet the ever-changing vision issues we face.

Fifteen years ago, I went in for an annual eye examination. After dilating the pupils of my eye, the optometrist asked a very startling question. "Did you know that you have cataracts?" I was surprised to hear this news. After all, I was only 45 years of age. I thought senior citizens were the ones who dealt with this challenge. He mentioned that the cataracts were small but reminded me to have them checked on a yearly basis.

This spring, I went in for my yearly exam, and the optometrist mentioned that the cataracts had grown, and I should consider having them removed. At first I thought, "Why should I go to all the trouble of having these cataracts removed? After all, I can see great with glasses." Or at least, that's what I was telling myself. When I would go to lunch and sit across a table looking at a person sitting against a window, their face was totally dark and unrecognizable. I had put up with this challenge for years and thought it was just the way things are.

The Doctor began to share about new advanced procedures that could not only remove my cataracts, but also insert a toric lense and remove my need for glasses.

Hearing this news seemed like a farfetched miracle as I have worn corrective glasses and contacts all my life. After prayer and discussing the issue with my wife, Debbie, I decided to go forward with cataract removal surgery following a planned motorcycle trip to New Jersey and back.

The procedure only lasted about 15 minutes. An incision was placed on top of the eye. A small instrument was placed inside the eye, and the doctor began to disintegrate the cataract. He then cauterized the wound and inserted a new toric lense into the area that once contained the cataract. The nurse taped my eyelid shut after the surgery, and Debbie took me home to rest. Six hours later, we were allowed to remove the tape from the eyelid. For the first time in my life, I could see perfectly out of my eye. I began to compare my vision with the other eye. It was like I was looking at a high definition television with the corrected eye and an old analog television with the uncorrected eye. The colors were exploding with brilliance. What looks grey through one eye, now looks brilliant white in the other. The definition of detail in tree leaves and even road signs are amazing. I suggested to Debbie that we take our motorcycle trip again so I could see the country in high definition.

The next day I went in for my post operation checkup. Guess what my vision is now? 20/20! To think that I could have gone through life never experiencing this kind of vision if it had not been for an annual checkup.

The same is true in ministry. Annual examinations are crucial for refocus. Below are lenses you can use to refocus your ministry vision on an annual basis.

IT IS AMAZING HOW EASILY WE CAN SLIDE BACK INTO AN INWARD-FOCUSED MENTALITY.

Below, are twelve outward-focused lenses leaders intending to lead an outward-focused church must constantly utilize. The lenses below will help you in your annual re-focusing sessions. These serve as a guide to readjust your focus.

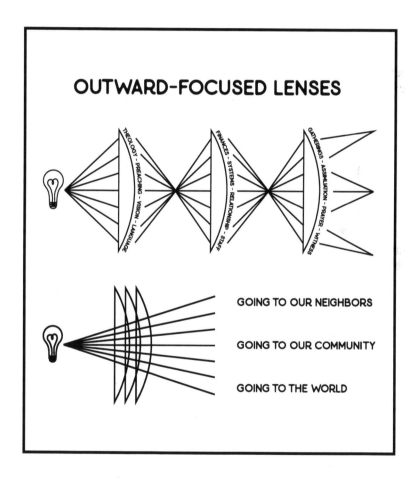

OUTWARD-FOCUSED THEOLOGY AND PREACHING

The mission of the church begins with the mission of God (*Missio Dei*). God calls the church to participate in His mission for the world and our communities. Outward-focused churches must be built on proper theology and preaching.

SOMEONE ONCE SAID, "YOU GET WHAT YOU PREACH FOR."

The church must be challenged to pursue the mission of God. This can take place in a number of ways, but the most effective approach is through preaching.

Pastors must communicate Jesus' mission, servanthood, and hospitality by being a voice of hope to the world.

So, as you study and prepare messages, look for outward-focused individuals and illustrations. The Bible is filled with people carrying out God's plan to reach out to all of the world with the Good News.

Also, preaching with proper theology and declaring the biblical purposes–discipleship, evangelism/outreach, instruction, fellowship, worship, service, and compassion–builds a dynamic ministry.

Believers are called to the mission of disciple-making and challenged to embrace a missionary identity, preferring the poor as a matter of Christ-centric ministry to society. Although not every Christian will become a fulltime missionary, they must adopt a missionary mindset.

CHRIST CHALLENGED THE TRADITIONAL INWARD-FOCUSED ATTITUDES OF RELIGION.

He encouraged the Church to live a life aware of the outsiders, seeking them out, living in compassion toward them, and offering a new life in Christ.

Another strategy outward-focused churches execute is to repeat their mission statements at least two to three times each service. This may seem difficult as you think about your ministry style, but it can happen in many forms. The biblical message will carry this theme, and your examples and application will support that as well.

Determine, in your prayerful preparation to preach or teach, how this lens will readjust your focus.

OUTWARD-FOCUSED VISION CASTING

It is a common practice to annually study a ministry's vision statement and adjust that in response to God's plan and the church's current condition. However, waiting for the annual evaluation can allow a church's vision to become out of focus if the lens is not adjusted periodically. There is a constant need for leadership to prayerfully seek God's vision for the weeks, months, and years ahead. It should go without saying, constant readjustment through the lens of vision casting is of utmost importance.

OUTWARD-FOCUSED VISION CASTING BEGINS WITH PRAYER AND COMES OUT OF A RELATIONSHIP WITH JESUS.

No shortcuts exist when it comes to prayer. Once a pastor has heard from the Lord concerning an outward-focused vision, he or she needs to encourage the congregation to pray passionately, without ceasing, for the addition of souls to the church, and ultimately the kingdom of God.

The lead pastor must lead the congregation in outward-focused vision casting. This can take place through weekend messages, social media like Twitter or Facebook, as well as an easily navigable updated website. Here is a great opportunity to use whatever means of communication church members access to strengthen the outward-focused vision.

Testimonies and stories combined with video and multi-media help to challenge the church to continue to look outward. Facilitate ways that outward-focused people can share their experience and heart with others. This helps people hear the same message from their peers, and from more than just the leadership of the church. This helps the vision become something obtainable and practical for all types of people. So seniors, youth, and even children can capture the vision you are trying to teach.

Lead pastors must communicate the vision to their staffs, teaching teams, ministry team leaders, and small group leaders. This is not a one-person vision. God has challenged lead pastors with a vision for the whole church. There will always be those who follow their team or group leader more than they follow the lead pastor. The connections and closeness that can develop in small groups or unique ministries can create followers who watch their specific leader in a dynamic way. Lead pastors multiply in effectiveness when the vision is understood and accepted by all of these team leaders.

Vision casting can also take place through sermon themes, community service, and training on outreach and evangelism. Pause and think through the recent sermon themes you have just preached. How did they underscore your outward-focused vision?

THE LEAD PASTOR SHOULD CHALLENGE THE CHURCH BODY TO THINK ABOUT MULTIPLICATION AND GROWTH AS NEW PEOPLE BEGIN A JOURNEY OF FAITH AND DISCIPLESHIP.

Many communities have special events that are seeking volunteers and involvement. Keep informed of news in the local paper, community bulletins, and neighborhood associations, as well as media announcements. We don't always have to create our own ministry events. There are countless opportunities to become a part of a community event with your church making a difference as they step outside your facility.

OUTWARD-FOCUSED LANGUAGE

Churches need to use proper language to transition into an outward-focused church. Think for a moment what the difference is between simply announcing "the events schedule for our seniors" and announcing "great events for all seniors." Additional prompts that encourage people to invite their neighbors using terms that verbally spark ideas for people to reach beyond the "regulars" are always important. Pastors are encouraged to create a glossary of terms for their church leaders and constituents.

ALL COMMUNICATION MUST ALIGN WITH THE CORE VALUES OF THE CHURCH.

The proper understanding of the definition of key words serve great importance. Your words can cause people to adjust their own verbiage and become more outward-focused.

The church needs to remove insider language and abbreviations that newcomers would not understand. When an event is announced in a certain location, do not assume everyone knows where that is located. Give added directions and be sure that building signage is clear as well. The larger your group of leadership is, the more you will have to instill the same language throughout the leadership team. Small group discussion guides can ensure everyone in the church learns the same outward-focused language and vision.

MEMBERS MUST CONSTANTLY LOOK THROUGH THE LENS OF A NEWCOMER AND SOMEONE WHO KNOWS NOTHING ABOUT CHRISTIANITY OR THE BIBLE, AND MAKE TERMS UNDERSTANDABLE.

Seekers appreciate speakers who can speak in their language and make them feel at home when they are new to the church. No one seeks out a place where they feel like an unwanted outsider.

Pastors and leaders, here is a simple challenge I encourage you to accept. Ask a solid leader from a nearby church to make a surprise, unremarked visit to your church. After their visit, use their input to evaluate how well newcomers are treated in your church. They will explain how it felt to enter your facility, the reactions of people, the clarity of signage, and the acceptance they felt in any ministry area.

This can also be a great way to see how your childrens ministries and youth programs receive newcomers. The same idea also applies to small groups, seniors events, and other special ministry settings.

You may also have another staff member set this up so that you are totally unaware of their reason for attending, so it can also be used to evaluate your speaking and responses as they relate to communicating an outward-focused mentality.

OUTWARD-FOCUSED FINANCES

Inward-focused churches tend to utilize all of their budget for building expenses and maintenance, programs for insiders, salaries, and benefits for staff. You may react by saying that these are critical parts of maintaining a church. That is true, but the key was the little word "all."

It has often been quoted, "You put your money where your heart is." This is especially true when we "give to God." But how would God spend your church budget? God's heart has always been outward-focused, so evaluate how much of your budget is focused on reaching out. This affects how you plan and budget your church finances. The budget is a reflection of the church's heart for the mission of God. What percentage of the budget is needed for an inwardly strong ministry? What percentage of the budget is directed toward both local missions and global missions? Is the budget in alignment with the mission of the church?

OUTWARD-FOCUSED MISSIONS STRATEGY

To lead an effective mission's ministry, the local church must have a mission's strategy. Many times, missions primarily takes place through relationships without much thought to the "why" of a mission's ministry in the church. People meet a missionary and add him or her to their giving budget, or they hear of a need in the community and develop a plan to help. They know what to do and even how to make it happen but the question needs to be "WHY?" If a church can develop their reasoning for having a mission's ministry around the "WHY," they can then go on to form the "WHAT" and "HOW" to make it successful.

The "WHY" should come back to the Great Commission; Jesus said to go! When the church believes this, they will want to go, and they will want to give. "WHAT companies do are external factors, but WHY they do it is something deeper."[52] Many churches today will have a missionary come and share for five minutes about their ministry. For some missionaries who are great communicators, this may work, but for many, it can miss the mark.

If the leadership of the church begins with the "WHY" before the missionary even takes the microphone, then the level of skill the missionary has in presenting their missions ministry in only five minutes is not important. The church leadership needs to be consistently explaining why the church has a mission's ministry. Jesus said to go to all the ends of the earth, and the church wants to fulfill that commandment, to reach not just those in our local communities but those around the world who do not know Jesus. And, in order to reach worldwide, the church believes in sending strategic partners who are called to foreign places.

We can't all go, but we can give, and we can pray. When people understand the "WHY," they will become passionate. The "WHY" brings urgency and a sense of belonging to something bigger than themselves. "We are drawn to leaders and organizations that are good at communicating what they believe. Their ability to make us feel like we belong, to make us feel special, safe and not alone is part of what gives them the ability to inspire us."[53] As the leadership communicates the "WHY," it brings clarity to mission's ministry. It isn't just another program of the Church; it is a commandment that must be fulfilled so that others may know Jesus.

A missions strategy should begin with these facets. Other strategies can be included to fit the culture of the local church.

OUTWARD-FOCUSED MISSIONS STRATEGY

FINANCES

TEACHING

LOCAL MISSIONS

GLOBAL MISSIONS

SHORT TERM MISSIONS TRIPS

DEVELOPING A COMPREHENSIVE OUTWARD-FOCUSED MISSIONS STRATEGY

Leading an effective mission's ministry in the local church, starts with developing a local church mission's strategy.

"A missions strategy is a comprehensive local and global missions plan for the church driven by the Biblical mission of God (*Missio Dei*) to bless all nations with the gospel incorporating the platinum circle and partnering with strategic partners for the greatest kingdom impact."

An Outward-Focused Missions Strategy lays out the HOW.

1. Develop a system of prayer for your strategic partners and Unreached People Groups
2. Establish a system of giving that includes both local and global missions
3. Communicate a biblical missions teaching platform for the church
4. Develop a Theology of Mission
5. Lead the way in developing Local Missions in bringing Compassion and the hope of Jesus to your community
6. Global Missions - Invite Strategic Mission Partners to share their stories and connect with the local church
7. Encourage your people to participate in short term Missions Trips both local and Global.

Although every missions strategy will most likely encompass all seven steps, the strategy must be unique to embody the outward-focused culture of every local church.

FINANCES

An outward-focused church budget must align with the church's mission. The budget is based on the church's values and biblical purposes. Global missions and local outreach budgets are often more than 20 percent of the general income of the church.

OUTWARD-FOCUSED CHURCHES ARE GENEROUS CHURCHES. THEY BELIEVE THAT BLESSING FOLLOWS OBEDIENCE TO GOD.

Many times outward-focused churches invite people to share in the vision and participate financially in the ministry of global partners and missionaries. This means there are opportunities to hear and respond to cross-cultural missionary needs as well as solid monthly reminders to be consistent in maintaining missionary pledges.

There are a number of ways that outward-focused churches communicate missions clearly in an ongoing way. Display areas, social media notices, short live or recorded reports from around the world, can all fill that void of silence when the schedule does not permit a full missions service. Many churches focus a lot of attention on annual missions emphasis. This can often result in heightened awareness and large fundraising opportunities, but when only mentioned once a year, this effect begins to fade quickly. Consider how newcomers can become involved and people can readjust their worldview throughout the entire year. Being outward-focused through missions requires more than just a once a year event.

THE CHURCH BECOMES A CONDUIT OF FINANCES FOR OUTREACH AND DISCIPLESHIP, VERSUS HOARDING FINANCES FOR A RAINY DAY.

There are some churches that do quite well at investing in missions. They have special fundraising for overseas work and support missionaries and missions agencies monthly. However, that same outward-focus for the world has yet to be translated into reaching out within their own country or even community.

OUTWARD-FOCUSED CHURCHES INVEST FINANCES IN OUTWARD-FOCUSED BRIDGE EVENTS TO ATTRACT NEWCOMERS.

If God's Word commands us to start our outward-focus right where we live, then we should see that as a major part of the church budget. Consider how many times and ways your church can reach out, and that will help you allocate funds for these bridges to reach people right in your own community. Many people may drive right by your building or even live within walking distance, but they have never been inside. Your outward-focused events will create a relational bridge for them to step into your facility. Use the lens of finances to strengthen your outward focus.

TEACHING

Teaching and instruction takes place in a variety of settings. In the weekend service, New Believers Class, Membership Class, Children's Ministries and Youth Ministries. This brings understanding and unity among the church attenders.

These teachings can include the theology of missions, missionary stories past and present, personal evangelism stories, whatever shows the "why" of the missions ministry: this church exists to share the good news of Jesus Christ here and abroad. This creates an urgency, an excitement that the church is on mission, and keeps the church looking outward and not becoming inward focus.

"The outward-focused church begins with building a solid theological foundation on God, which includes His desire to reach out and bless humankind. These churches possess a theology of mission, believing God is a missionary God."[54] This moves missions from program to passion. It is "why" the church exists. For there to be a mission's strategy for the church, the church must understand the importance of missions to the church both local and abroad.

The church cannot expect a missionary with a five-minute window to convey a missional theology to the church. This is the responsibility of the leadership to make sure it is being taught throughout the church. Within this teaching, there must be the encouragement for each person to ask God where they fit on this spectrum. Are they to go or are they to send?

We need to be encouraging the next generation to answer the call, giving instruction and input that can help them on this journey. If an attender of a church is asked if the church has a mission's ministry, they should be able to confidently answer the "why" of their mission's ministry and the "how" and "what" of accomplishing local and global missions in their church. This shouldn't be a program shrouded with mystery and lack of understanding; it should be the ministry that leads the church.

LOCAL MISSIONS

A mission's strategy includes local missions. This should include community projects, personal evangelism, and big events; anything that reaches out or gives to the local community. This is where it is important to be involved in and develop relationships with community leaders in the local area. Letting the church have a presence in the community that is positive, uplifting, and encouraging, brings goodwill to the church and opens the doors of the church to those who need Jesus.

The leadership needs to remember the "why" of the church when reaching out into the community. Many times churches will do great things in the community but never get beyond showing the love part. Any organization can do this. The church needs to take it to the next level by explaining why they love: to share Jesus. Starting conversations, sharing a testimony, or inviting the person to church, needs to be as important as the event. If the "why" isn't kept at the front of all these great endeavors, and no one comes to find Jesus Christ as their personal Savior, the church will experience a lot of accolades from the community, but that doesn't accomplish the Great Commission. At this point, it becomes more about what people are thinking about the church than about Jesus Christ.

Once the "why" is established, the leadership must decide on the best options for local missions and the percentage of finances that will be allotted towards each ministry.

In the area of personal evangelism, it is important to share the stories. If a person comes to find Christ, have them share their testimony on video and run it during service time. These stories encourage the church and help others see the possibilities of what they can do in their place of influence.

Part of a mission's strategy should be water baptisms. When there is a baptismal, make it exciting, a celebration of a new life in Christ. Our home church, The Grove, does an excellent job in this area: families getting baptized, parents baptizing their children, pastors and friends baptizing someone they were crucial in leading to Jesus. These experiences remind the church of the "why:" making disciples here and abroad.

Locally, the church must take advantage of the mission field being at their front door. How can the local church reach out to the ethnic minorities in their own area? How can the local church have ethnic diversity? Author Erwin McManus states that it begins with the leadership making friends with people who are different than themselves, modeling diverse friendships.

If your goal is a diverse church, then you need to ask God to give you a love for people who are different from you. People go to church where they have friends or make friends. You can't expect people who are different from you to come to church simply because you want to paint a picture of diversity. This only happens when love actually brings people together. This must start with leadership and flow down through every area of the church.[55]

GLOBAL MISSIONS

Global Missions includes guest missionaries, resident missionaries, mission's projects–such as orphanages and water programs–and developing a missionary pipeline to send people from the local church. Many times missionaries are invited due to a relationship or connection to the church, but what if a church looked at the globe, and strategically tried to reach each continent or people group, and began selecting those missionaries to supports from this perspective. Or maybe a church chooses one continent that will be their focal point for projects and then support various missionaries throughout the world. Many times it is left to the leadership to field phone calls and pick a missionary when the time is right - or when the church is having a mission's convention.

What if the leadership had a strategic plan and then called missionaries asking them to come as their strategic partners to share what God is doing in their part of the world? This would follow the Apostle Paul's example after his first missionary trip. He returned to Antioch and shared what God was doing in the foreign lands. This encouraged the people of Antioch as they heard what was happening across the globe. Similarly, churches can encourage their people by sharing what is happening on the church's invovlment with missions in-person or on video.

Another great option is having a resident missionary be a part of the local church. When a missionary is in the States, encourage them to make your church their home base. Attending the church when they don't have services, being treated like church staff, having a place where they belong creates a two fold win: it helps the missionary family connect and feel included, plus it helps those in the local church to identify with and come to know a missionary family up close. This kind of relationships takes down the walls of "them and us" and allows the "we" to form, a rich relationship that will continue for many years. It will develop the culture of having strategic partners abroad.

Many churches currently do mission's projects overseas: helping to build something, get clean water to a village, orphanages, provide health and dental clinics, and the list continues. There are so many areas in which a church can give financially and make a difference. Once again, the church needs to come back to their "why" and understand that if there is not a connection with a missionary or national pastor, the church is helping people but not giving an opportunity for that person to be in contact with someone who can ultimately lead them to Jesus. It is important for churches to look closely at each opportunity and make sure they are legitimate and will give help to the already established missionaries. This is where stewards of God's money must make wise decisions, partnering with organizations like Assemblies of God World Missions, that share the same "why" in missions as the church.

Finally, as previously discussed, the church must be teaching the next generation about the theology of missions and giving them opportunity to follow God's leading in their own lives. The church needs to be preparing the next generation to go into all the world and preach the gospel. This can be done with teaching, personal coaching/mentoring, and allowing times of honest discussions. A great example would be having an open format with missionaries during which youth can ask questions and have opportunity to see what Assemblies of God World Missions does with MAPS and other programs. This is the ultimate outward-focused church—one that is preparing and sending the next generation.

SHORT TERM MISSIONS' TRIPS

Short term missions trips come in several forms. Short term mission's trips include working trips where a group builds or works in some type of project that helps a community or ministry. Also included are mission's trips that take a group of people who are called to missions, whether through sending or going, and letting them experience missions on the ground level, spending time with missionaries and their churches, and seeing what they are doing to fulfill the Great Commission. This would include a financial blessing for the missionary to thank them for their hospitality. It is interesting to see if these types of mission's trips help with mission's giving in the local church. People want to have adventure, so finding a way to take a personal mission's trip that would help define the "why" towards the mission's ministry in the local church could bring great benefits.

If a church wants to stay outward-focused, it must prioritize having a mission's strategy.

OUTWARD-FOCUSED RELATIONSHIPS

Relationship building is critical to an outward-focused church. Church attendees build relationships as they participate in activities and ministries designed to reach out to new people–the unbelieving, unchurched, de-churched and potential attendees. The majority of new people who step into an outward-focused church received an invitation by a friend or relative.

Outward-focused churches understand God has called them to live missional lives and continually step out of their comfort zones, building relationships with people with whom they live, work, and play.

OUTWARD-FOCUSED CHURCHES UNDERSTAND GOD HAS CALLED THEM TO LIVE MISSIONAL LIVES.

Outward-focused churches strategize how they can get to know civic leaders by joining the fire department, police department, school boards, emergency services, town hall, and sports activities.

Outward-focused churches spend money and time investing in building relationships with pre-Christians. Pastors challenge every church attendee to reach their sphere of influence, recognizing that family, friends, neighbors, and people they meet are their mission field.

Every member of your church needs to understand that their job, the neighborhood where they live, and the people they do business with, are opportunities to build relationships with a purpose. Children and youth must understand that every relationship opportunity is an opportunity that can be used by God.

Some churches spend large amounts of money on church flyers or invite cards that can be stuck on people's doors. This may result in someone visiting a church, and it certainly is one way of gaining some visibility. But the most effective way of reaching people is to have outward-focused members who understand the power of relational outreach. A hand delivered invitation means so much more than a generic invitation with no connecting relationship.

OUTWARD-FOCUSED STAFF

Lead pastors must encourage existing staff to become outward focused. This will take time and energy on your part, but it will help you create the outward-focused atmosphere that needs to permeate every ministry. This can all change when new staff is added as well. When hiring staff, strive to find outward-focused, friendly leaders, and schedule regular times with them to emphasize prayer for outsiders. You want to keep this focus intentional.

Lead pastors should encourage staff to read outward-focused books and articles together and to know their neighbors, possessing a passion for the Great Commission. People will be watching for outward-focus ministry to be modeled by leadership.

OUTWARD-FOCUSED PUBLIC GATHERINGS

Outward-focused public gatherings remove as many distractions and hindrances as possible in order for a first-time guest to encounter Jesus Christ. These are events that step outside the church facility to engage people who have not or will not enter that building. Parks, schools, auditoriums, and even parking lots can be used to create a public space that is more acceptable to some people. The truth is, a church building can be a distraction for those unaccustomed to attending church, and a hindrance for those who have been hurt or are disillusioned by a church.

Holding events in a neutral community setting allows people to meet believers, be served by believers, and hear the love of God that believers want to extend to a lost and hurting society. I am reminded of an entire family that attended a church sponsored Easter Egg Hunt in a nearby park. The father of the family was a prominent banker who just couldn't believe people would do this for free for his kids. That was what opened the door for their family to start attending the church. In time, that family became one of the core families of the church, and numerous years later, he left banking and joined the church staff as an associate pastor. Unsurprisingly, that church is sold on bridge-building public gatherings!

There is also a need to create some of those options during the main church service. Churches design weekend services as outward-focused, friendly gatherings, by utilizing such things as adequate parking, inviting lobby experiences, and even common dress and clothing. This can also mean unique schedules that better fit the people the church is trying to reach.

This can also affect how the church service is structured. Timeframe, service components, and style can also create or hinder an outward-focused environment. There will always be a variety of music styles and preferences. Every pastor has been made painfully aware that not everyone would choose the style they are using. The question is not which style is most popular or which one makes the fewest people unhappy. The style process should reflect what is the most effective demonstration of being outward-focused to reach new people with the message of God's love.

MUSIC STYLES RELATE MORE TO THE NEW PEOPLE THE CHURCH IS REACHING RATHER THAN INSIDERS' PERSONAL PREFERENCES.

Outward-focused gatherings should take place regularly to reach out into the community. Make this a regular part of your church planning. Get events on the calendar and see if that includes more than a once a year favorite activity that everyone is tired of doing.

Yes, even great ideas need to be adjusted, adapted, and changed from time to time. Attention spans seem short in children, but if we are honest, they are also short with church people.

The first year an event is planned it may take time for your people to catch the vision and get involved. The second year they understand the concept better and more people are helping and more people attend. But by the third year, the interest starts to fade, and much time beyond that, you have no one that wants to be involved. If this sounds familiar, join the crowd. Today things change quickly and constantly. We need to try fresh ideas and readjust public events to spark the interest of both church volunteers and the community we are reaching.

These public events may include community trunk or treat, hosting business groups, financial peace university, exercise classes, divorce recovery classes, twelve-step groups, and preschool options. There is an endless list of creative ways ministries are being outward-focused through public gatherings.

When it comes to public gatherings, a "customer service" culture must be noticeable. During our motorcycle trip across America, we could identify which restaurants, hotels and Harley Shops believed in customer service. If there is one organization in the community that should excel in customer service, it is the Church.

IF THERE IS ONE ORGANIZATION IN THE COMMUNITY THAT SHOULD EXCEL IN CUSTOMER SERVICE, IT IS THE CHURCH.

I noticed that those who were trained in customer service stopped what they were doing when I entered the room. They immediately gave eye contact and asked a simple question, "How can I help you," and "How is your day going?" Once they took care of my needs they would follow up with a question like, "Is there anything else I can do for you today?"

Outward-focused churches begin in the parking lot. Guests arrive with the feeling that this church is ready for "new company." Parking lot greeters all have fluorescent vests on, and with excitement, guide everyone to the parking spots. In the Pacific Northwest, when it rains, people are encouraged to drop off their passengers at the door and umbrellas are made available.

OUTWARD-FOCUSED ASSIMILATION

Assimilation is the process of blending newcomers into the church body. Outward-focused churches generally use an assimilation system. Every church should consider a feedback loop for visitors. Somehow you should find out answers to these questions:

· Did you find everything you were looking for?

· What do we do that you don't particularly like?

- Is there anything else we could have done to have made your time with us better?

- What do we do well that would cause you to return?

- Would you recommend us to your best friend and loved ones? If yes, why? If not, why not?

The church can learn how to treat guests by studying the example of businesses and business leaders who excel in customer service. The leading business that excels in customer service is the Ritz-Carlton Hotel Company. Joseph A. Michelli is the author of the book, *The New Gold Standard.* Michelli shares five leadership principles for creating a legendary customer experience.[56] The five principals are:

- Define and refine

- Empower through trust

- It's not about you

- Deliver the wow!

- Leave a lasting footprint

Every employee of the Ritz Carlton is empowered with a monthly budget to take care of the urgent needs of their guests.

Friends of mine, Tom and Lori, experienced this firsthand at a recent conference we hosted at a Ritz Carlton. On the opening day of the conference, the event coordinator at the Ritz stopped by the registration table to ask if there was anything she could do for them. Lori happened to mention her son, Austin, was running a half-marathon in Springfield, Missouri that day. Later, the coordinator stopped by again to inquire about the outcome after Lori had just received a text that Austin had actually won the half-marathon. The coordinator was very kind and generous with her congratulations.

Because of their leadership responsibilities, Tom and Lori were not able to make it back to their room until late that night. They opened the door to find a framed photo of Austin crossing the finish line along with his half-marathon time, a card of congratulations signed by the staff, and a beautifully presented (and delicious!) tray of gourmet chocolate prepared by the Ritz chef to celebrate their son's accomplishment. It was amazing!

One of the best ways to improve customer service in the church is by encouraging the leaders to improve their listening skills. People appreciate those who show their concern through listening. In a day of social media, people can often be distracted from communicating with the ones they are with. There are many who have never learned the art of listening. In the book, *The Customer Rules*, Lee Cockerell shares some tips on practicing the art of listening.[57]

- Get into the right position to listen. By that I mean speak to the customer in a quiet location where you will not be distracted.

- Give the customer your full attention. Maintain eye contact. Don't interrupt. Don't multitask. Don't show any signs of impatience or distraction with your body language.

- If possible, take notes. Don't count on remembering everything that was said.

- Give the speaker a chance to finish before you reply. You might even ask, is there anything else you would like to tell me?" before responding.

- When the customer is finished speaking, reiterate or paraphrase what he or she said.

- Once you verify what was said, ask additional questions to improve your understanding.

- At every step, make the customer feel valued and appreciated.

- And for goodness' sake, if you receive a complaint, apologize. Saying you're sorry can be the best way for customers to feel you care.

Quality customer service in the Church should begin with developing system of assimilation. Nelson Searcy sells an excellent assimilation system called Fusion. Fusion incorporates the use of investigation, invitation, integration and incorporation. There are many assimilation systems to choose from so you don't have to invent your own. A true outward-focused church connects new people with those in the church who may have some type of affinity with the guest. Assimilation helps to lead people in discovering others in the church who have common interests and hobbies.

ASSIMILATION IS THE PROCESS OF BLENDING NEWCOMERS INTO THE CHURCH BODY.

To blend newcomers with existing members, you have to begin researching interest groups that already connect some of the people in your church. Leaders need to be listening for this. It calls for your attention and willingness to think outside the box, or as some would say, outside the church.

One church found that a number of men enjoyed working on cars. These men started to meet informally at car shows and each guy invited a friend to come along. They even took this outward-focused idea further when some of the men began to ask God how they could serve others using this interest. Now every spring and fall, those men hold a free clinic out in the parking lot for single moms and widows throughout the community. They change the oil, check the engine, and prepare for winter and summer auto needs. They have done some minor repairs or assisted women whose cars are unsafe or in need of help. These men, both regular church goers and interested friends, have discovered a way to make a loving impact on the community using their skills and interest.

These same assimilation groups can grow out of many service opportunities like community projects, food banks, soup kitchens, and schools. These can be ways to help people build relationships with others of like passion.

Another factor in assimilation is the actual follow up process that helps you retain new people. There are software programs, communication styles, and ministry groups that can all help design ways to make this happen. But the first step is being aware that this is a critical factor that every church must deal with. Many non-attenders today will say they went to church before, but when they quit going, no one seemed to notice or care. An outward-focused church shows that they care.

ASSIMILATION IS THE ART OF FOLLOWING UP WITH NEW, FIRST-TIME GUESTS, WITH THE EMPHASIS OF ENCOURAGING THEM TO RETURN AND BUILD RELATIONSHIPS WITH OTHERS AS SOON AS POSSIBLE.

OUTWARD-FOCUSED PRAYER

Pastors are to help churched people identify unchurched people who God has placed in their paths to discover, trust, and love. This will take training and time to develop this outward-focused way of looking at people. They should be encouraged often to develop and maintain a prayer list, praying daily for the non-Christian friends.

Prayer lists can be effective ways to focus ahead, especially during special holiday seasons. Christmas and Easter are the two easiest days of the year to get some people to come to church. But there may be a Fourth of July event, a community outdoor gathering, or another special time when those within the church can make fresh prayer lists to pray for and then invite the unchurched.

The church can rally behind special times of prayer that are outward-focused, experience God's special, moving power when they pray in an focused manner together. Personal prayer reminders, like notecards, flyers, bookmarks, or media blasts, will encourage people toward outward-focused praying.

Don't forget to include children and youth in this lens. They too need to develop an outward-focus and can be powerful prayer warriors. Their peers will often respond to them rather than an adult with whom have no relationship.

OUTWARD-FOCUSED PRAYER MEETINGS ARE ENCOURAGED, WHERE EVERYTHING PRAYED ABOUT IN THAT MEETING IS OUTWARD-FOCUSED.

Outward-focused prayer also involves praying for missionaries who are team members overseas. They count on the church joining them through prayer to reach people with the Gospel. This reminds the church that we must adjust our vision to focus both at home and abroad.

OUTWARD-FOCUSED SPIRITUAL EMPOWERMENT

Leaders must accept the challenge to create an outward-focused church. The task can be started in a ministry but can also become routine and forgotten after time passes. The need to stay fresh and effective in our focus is constant, and the power needed to make that happen has been provided for us. The final lens through which we readjust our outward-focus comes through the empowerment of the Holy Spirit.

THE EMPOWERMENT OF THE HOLY SPIRIT IS CRITICAL IN HAVING OUTWARD-FOCUSED SUCCESS.

Maybe you have tried the previous 10 lenses. You have brought in new staff, new ideas, new style, and new thinking. You have prayerfully worked through the process of refocusing your church, and you are now wondering how it can be so easy to slide back toward inward-focused thinking. Outward-focused churches are encouraged in scripture to preach, teach, and encourage believers to receive the empowerment of the Holy Spirit as mentioned in Acts 1:8.

VISION CHECK

1. How long has it been since your church or ministry made major changes? What were those changes?

2. Which of the ten lenses is most needed to readjust your church now?

3. How do you communicate vision? In what ways do you do vision casting?

4. What terminology do you and your staff use to encourage outward focus?

5. What would you say are the top 3 ways your church uses finances and volunteers for outward focused events?

Conclusion

When it comes to being outward-focused, the ultimate Helper will always be the Holy Spirit. You may need to pause and stroll back through Scripture to see that rough-around-the-edges fisherman named Peter, denied he even knew Jesus. He probably reflects many of us in our weaknesses and struggles to do what God has called us to do. Then we see him addressing the multitude in Acts 2, and marvel at the skillful way thousands responded to the Gospel.

We all need that boldness, that keen awareness of God's plan, that power that helps us truly see the love of God that is there for a lost and dying world. Suddenly our eyes are readjusted from being inward-focused upon our own selfish needs to being outward-focused, accomplishing God's ultimate purpose.

Moving a church from an inward-focused culture to an outward-focused culture does not guarantee that all your problems will be removed. On the contrary, pastors and leaders must prepare for the push back from a congregation when you ask them to move out of the status quo. Remember that you are not walking this journey alone. This is Christ's mission, and He has given you the counselor and comforter through the person of the Holy Spirit to empower you for every challenge.

I recommend leaders take a spiritual retreat each year in order for the pastor to get away from all the voices and learn to hear Jesus' voice. Pastors will have difficulty listening to Jesus' voice unless they periodically unplug from all of their electrical devices and get away with just Jesus and His Word. Many voices daily bombard leaders, trying to buy for their time and focus. Jesus' voice is an outward-focused voice. Like a shepherd, He is not content until all His sheep are saved.

If a man has a hundred sheep, and one of them has gone astray, does he not leave the ninety-nine on the mountains and go and search for the one that is straying? If it turns out that he finds it, truly I say to you, he rejoices over it more than over the ninety-nine, which have not gone astray. Therefore, it is not the will of your Father who is in heaven that one of these little ones perish (Matt. 18:12-14).

A renewed Holy Spirit empowerment brings a fresh ability to listen to Jesus' voice.

Never stop examining what you and your ministry are doing. Join me in the lifelong pursuit of seeing, with His outward-focused eyes, the field that is ripe for harvest.

Endnotes

ENDNOTES

INTRODUCTION

1. Thom Rainer, *I Am a Church Member: Discovering the Attitude That Makes the Difference* (Nashville: B & H Publishing Group, 2013), 16.

CHAPTER 1 - OUT OF FOCUS

2. Peter Greer, *Mission Drift : The Unspoken Crisis Facing Leaders, Charities, and Churches* (Minneapolis, Minnesota: Bethany House Publishers, a division of Baker Publishing Group, 2014), 72.

3. Gary McIntosh, *There's Hope for Your Church : First Steps to Restoring Health and Growth* (Grand Rapids, MI: Baker Books, 2012), 20.

4. JR Woodward, *Creating a Missional Culture: Equipping the Church for the Sake of the World* (Intervaristy Press, 2012), 20, Kindle.

5. Thom Rainer, *I Am a Church Member: Discovering the Attitude That Makes the Difference* (Nashville Tennessee: B & H Publishing Group, 2013), 11.

6. David T. Olson, *The American Church in Crisis* (Grand Rapids, MI: Zondervan, 2008), 246-248, Kindle.

7. Thom Rainer, 17.

8. Peter Greer and Chris Horst, *Mission Drift: The Unspoken Crisis Facing Leaders, Charities, and Churches* (Baker Publishing Group, 2014), 72, Kindle.

9. John A. Shedd, Goodreads, https://www.goodreads.com/author/quotes/5171938.John_A_Shedd. Accessed 2/03/2018.

CHAPTER 2 - OUT OF FOCUS

10. Simon Sinek, *Start with Why: How Great Leaders Inspire Everyone to Take Action* (New York: Portfolio, 2009), 37.

11. Ibid., 37.

12. Gary McIntosh and Charles Arn, *What Every Pastor Should Know : 101 Indispensable Rules of Thumb for Leading Your Church* (Grand Rapids: Baker Books, 2013), 14.

13. All Scripture references, unless otherwise noted, are from the New International Version.

CHAPTER 3 - EXAMINING FOCUS

14. George O. Wood, "Compassionate Christ, Comassionate Church," *Enrichment Journal* Winter 2012 (2012): 26.

15. Ibid., 27.

16. Ibid., 27.

17. Richard Schoonover, "Compassion Ministry: Expressing the Heart of God," *Enrichment Journal* Winter 2012 (2012): 25.

18. "MissionInsite Products for Churches" http://missioninsite.com/ (accessed 06/06/2014).

CHAPTER 4 - ADJUSTING FOCUS

19. Edgar H. Schein, *Organizational Culture and Leadership*, 4th ed. (San Francisco: Jossey-Bass, 2010), 7.

20. Andy Stanley, *Deep & Wide: Creating Churches Unchurched People Love to Attend* (Grand Rapids, MI: Zondervan, 2012), 302-306, Kindle.

21. Reccommended resource: "Crucial Cultural Questions." found in the Refocus Workbook.

22. William R. Hoyt, *Effectiveness by the Numbers: Counting What Counts in the Church* (Nashville: Abingdon Press, 2007), 316-323, Kindle.

23. Schein, 321, Kindle.

24. Ibid., 582.

25. Larry Bossidy, Ram Charan, and Charles Burck, *Execution : The Discipline of Getting Things Done, 1st ed.* (New York: Crown Business, 2002), 24.

26. Michael A. Beitler, *Strategic Organizational Change : A Practitioner's Guide for Managers and Consultants*, 3rd ed. (Greensboro: Practitioner Press International, 2013), 39.

27. Ibid., 40.

28. John P. Kotter, Leading Change (Boston, Mass.: Harvard Business Review Press, 2012), 42.

29. C.S. Lewis, Mere Christianity. (Macmillan, 1952), Book II, Chapter 3.

30. John P. Kotter, *Leading Change* (Boston, Mass.: Harvard Business Review Press, 2012), 3.

31. Ibid., 37.

32. Ibid., 45.

33. Beitler, 41.

34. Kotter, 58.

35. Beitler, 43.

36. Kotter, 70.

37. Ibid., 91.

38. Beitler, 46.

39. Ibid., 46.

40. Kotter, 125.

41. Ibid., 127.

42. Beitler, 47.

43. Kotter, 154.

44. Beitler, 48.

45. Kotter, 164.

46. Ibid., 165.

CHAPTER 5 - OUTWARD-FOCUSED

47. Ibid., 846, Kindle.

48. Ibid., 167, Kindle.

49. Dino Rizzo, *Servolution: Starting a Church Revolution through Serving (Leadership Network Innovation Series)* (Grand Rapids, MI: Zondervan, 2009), 25, Kindle.

50. Guder, 1020, Kindle.

51. Ibid., 1638, Kindle.

52. Simon Sinek, *Start with Why* (New York, NY, Penguin Group, 2009), 41.

53. Ibid., 55.

54. Ed Stetzer, *Planting Missional Churches: Planting a Church That's Biblically Sound and Reaching People in Culture* (Nashville: Broadman & Holman, 2006), 20.

55. Erwin Raphael McManus, *An Unstoppable Force* (Orange, California: Yates and Yates), 54-55.

56. Joseph Michelli, *The New Gold Standard: 5 Leadership Principles for Creating a Legendary Customer Experience Courtesy of the Ritz-Carlton Hotel Company* (McGraw-Hill Education, 2008), Kindle.

57. Lee Cockerell, *The Customer Rules: The 39 Essential Rules for Delivering Sensational Service* (New York, NY: The Crown Publishing Group, 2008), 918-921, Kindle.

ADDITIONAL RESOURCES

RESOURCES BY DR. DAVE E. COLE

Additional resources available from the Outward-Focused Network.

WHAT THE CHURCH CAN LEARN FROM HARLEY DAVIDSON

REFOCUS - OUTWARD-FOCUSED JOURNEY WORKBOOK

Learn more at www.outwardfocused.com

OUTWARD-FOCUSED CHURCH SEMINARS:

Learn more at www.outwardfocused.com